WHITNEY HOUSTON
THE GREATEST LOVE OF ALL

Written by

Carolyn McHugh

sona
BOOKS

sona BOOKS

First Published Danann Media Publishing 2022

WARNING: For private domestic use only, any unauthorised Copying, hiring,
lending or public performance of this book is illegal.

CAT NO: SON0491

Photography courtesy of

Getty images:

Georges De Keerle
Ian Showell/Keystone
Jack Mitchell
Doug Vann/Corbis
Paul Natkin
Galuschka/ullstein bild
Michael Ochs Archives
Lester Cohen
Dirck Halstead
Michael Putland
Gideon Mendel/Corbis
Bill Marino/Sygma

Graham Wiltshire
Chu Ming-hoi/South China Morning Post
Mike Slaughter/Toronto Star
L. Cohen/WireImage
Ron Galella Collection
Michael Zagaris
Robin Platzer
Sonia Moskowitz
George Pimentel/WireImage
Rita Barros
Paul Bergen/Redferns
20th Century Fox

Fotos International
Larry Busacca/WireImage
JMEnternational
Jeff Kravitz/FilmMagic
Brigitte Engl/Redferns
Scott Gries/ImageDirect
Gina Ferazzi/Los Angeles Times
M. Caulfield/WireImage
Frank Micelotta/ImageDirect
Don Arnold/WireImage

Alamy:

Colaimages
Album
Landmark Media
MediaPunch Inc

Blueee
Everett Collection Inc
TCD/Prod.DB
Entertainment Pictures

Maximum Film
PictureLux/The Hollywood Archive
Sipa US

Other images, Wiki Commons

Book design Darren Grice at Ctrl-d
Copy editor Juliette O'Neill

Made in EU.
ISBN: 978-1-912918-58-4

Contents

Born to sing

I f ever a child was born to sing it was surely Whitney Houston. Her mother was the successful gospel/R&B singer Cissy Houston who backed stars including Frank Sinatra and Elvis Presley; her cousin was 1960s pop and soul star Dionne Warwick; and her godmother, dubbed the 'Queen of Soul', was Aretha Franklin.

But that is not to suggest that Whitney had it easy with a career handed to her on a plate. Fame and commercial success – her own and that of her talented relatives – still had to be hard won in 1960s America. Racial tensions were high as black Americans sought their civil rights and African Americans were only just beginning to break barriers and make their mark in the entertainment industry.

Born in the industrial city of Newark, New Jersey, USA on 9 August 1963, Whitney Elizabeth Houston was the youngest of the three children of Cissy and John Houston. Her two older brothers were Gary and Michael. Gary was actually a half-brother, eight years her senior, from Cissy's first marriage, but John brought him up as one of his own. Cissy's first marriage had ended in divorce a few months before Gary was born in 1957. Cissy and John were together for several years, and had Michael and Whitney, before they married, following John's own divorce in 1964.

John Houston Jr. was an Army veteran who had served in the Second World War. He was working as a driver when he met Cissy in 1958 after her divorce, but shortly after that he began his own career in the entertainment business. He first managed vocal group The Gospelaires, and then throughout the 1960s he managed Cissy's group The Sweet Inspirations.

During times when Cissy was away working, John would happily stay at home and look after the children. Whitney adored him.

In 1967, following a difficult period of race riots in Newark, the family relocated to the slightly less tough neighbourhood of East Orange, New Jersey. Whitney was four and a happy child, if a little shy. As the only girl and the baby of the family, Whitney was rather indulged by her father who nicknamed her 'Nippy' – a name which stuck and can be seen on the back of her first album on a list of some personal 'thank yous'.

Her family was close, loving and godly and Whitney grew up in a home full of song and creative energy. Her mother Cissy had worked in a recording studio until late into her pregnancy and so, from her time in the womb, Whitney had been exposed to the sound of music.

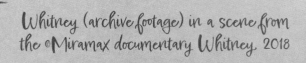

Whitney (archive footage) in a scene from the ©Miramax documentary Whitney, 2018

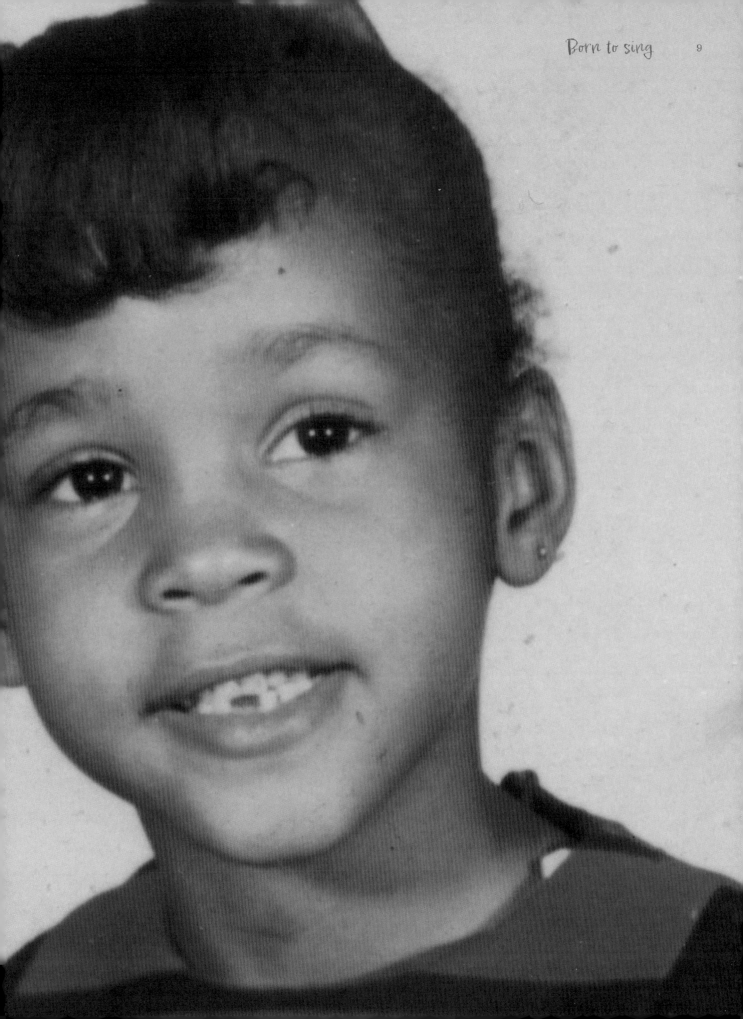

Whitney said she could remember singing from about the age of five. It seemed to come naturally to her and she, along with many others, believed her voice was a gift from God. 'When I started singing, it was almost like speaking.... something that's inside of you,' she said later. 'You just know.'

As a child dreaming of her future Whitney considered becoming a teacher, then a vet. But as soon as she realised she had a voice unlike any other, she knew where her destiny lay.

As she told Rolling Stone magazine in a 1993 interview; 'By the age of ten or eleven, when I opened my mouth and said, "Oh, God, what's this?" I kind of knew teaching and being a veterinarian were gonna have to wait. What's in your soul is in your soul.

The first time I sang in church I knew that this was something God had given me and that he wanted me to use'

The family were very involved with their local church, New Hope Baptist Church, where Cissy led the music programme.

Encouraged by her mother, Whitney began performing as a soloist in the junior gospel choir and made her solo debut, aged 11, singing 'Guide Me, O Thou Great Jehovah'. Whitney remembered being scared and aware of everybody staring at her like they were in a trance. 'When I finished everyone clapped and started crying. From then on I knew God had blessed me.

My mother always said to me. 'If you don't feel it, then don't mess with it, because it's a waste of time'.

But young Whitney did 'feel it'. 'I grew up in the church, and gospel music has always been the centre of our lives', she said. 'It taught me a lot about singing. It gave me emotion and spiritual things and it helped me to know what I was singing about, because in gospel music the words mean everything. Now whatever I sing, whether it's gospel or pop or R&B, I feel it. I think I got my emotion from gospel singing, from my mom instilling it in me at an early age. You can't make people feel anything you don't feel yourself. Memories of singing in church are ones I cherish the most.'

Whitney's brother Gary can remember a young Whitney playing at being a star, singing in the basement of their house, dressed in one of her mother's gowns
.
Outside of church Whitney also had a chance to see what singing professionally was like when

she accompanied her mother at work in a recording studio or performing on stage. Cissy often worked with Aretha Franklin, who Whitney knew as her 'Auntie Ree'. Then of course she watched her older cousins, Dionne Warwick and Dee Dee Warwick, make their name in the charts. She even had a second cousin on Cissy's side who was a famous soprano opera singer, Leontyne Price. The musical genes were definitely within her in abundance.

Multi-Grammy award-winner Dionne was the most famous of the family at that time, enjoying phenomenal success throughout the 1960s, most notably with Burt Bacharach numbers. Her huge hits include the classic songs 'I Say a Little Prayer', 'That's What Friends Are For' and 'Do You Know the Way to San Jose?'

Whitney's other cousin Dee Dee, who was Dionne's sister, also enjoyed some recording success herself. Although she never reached the heights of her sister and cousin, Dionne and Whitney, she did make the charts in the 1960s several times, including with the original version of 'I'm Gonna Make You Love Me' – later a bigger hit for The Supremes.

So having seen such success at close quarters, realising she had a beautiful voice of her own, recognising her dazzling pedigree and having soaked up the atmosphere of studios and theatres from birth,

it was perhaps no surprise that Whitney took to singing as she did

Whitney (archive footage) in a scene from
the Miramax documentary Whitney, 2018

I learned from the best

Whitney never failed to acknowledge the important part her mother Cissy played in starting and steering her career. 'The sounds in my house were gospel. I'm a singer because of her,' she said. 'My mother was my first example that I looked at and said, "Wow, that voice right there." And I'm her daughter, so I sound like my mother when my mother was my age, though I truly think my mother has a greater voice than me, because she's the master, I'm the student. She has greater range, greater power than I ever did.'

There is no doubt that Cissy 'made' Whitney – and in fact enabled her daughter to have the career that she would have liked for herself

It was frustrating for Cissy that fame as a solo artist had eluded her. Although she spent three decades as a well-respected and sought-after gospel, soul and pop singer, working with many of the greatest names in the business, including Frank Sinatra, Elvis Presley and Aretha Franklin, she was always the 'bridesmaid' rather than the 'bride' in terms of success as a solo artist. But her versatile, cross-genre style meant that she always worked and had fantastic knowledge of her craft and the music industry knowledge to share with Whitney.

Cissy was born Emily Drinkard in Newark, New Jersey, on 30 September 1933, the youngest of eight children. Her singing career began as part of her family gospel group The Drinkard Four, alongside her brothers Larry and Nicky and sister Ann. This later evolved to become The Drinkard Singers and include her sister Lee Warwick, who was the mother of Dionne and Dee Dee Warwick – the sisters both changed the spelling of their surname to Warwick as a stage name. The Drinkard Singers were particularly successful in the late 1950s and recorded a live album for RCA called '*A Joyful Noise*'.

Then in 1963 Cissy began the four-strong female vocal group Sweet Inspirations, whose other original members were her nieces Dionne and Dee Dee Warwick, both then in their early 20s and only some 10 years younger than Cissy. The fourth member of the group was Doris Troy who had worked with the Warwick sisters as a backing vocalist at Atlantic Records. The group enjoyed great success, providing back-up vocals for leading artists of the time including Otis Redding, Wilson Pickett, The Drifters and Dusty Springfield. In 1969 the group sang backing vocals for Elvis Presley when he made his legendary comeback performances in Las Vegas.

Sweet Inspirations (left to right): Cissy Drinkard Houston, Myrna Smith, Sylvia Shemwell and Estelle Brown

But by now Cissy had had her children and was finding that she no longer enjoyed spending long periods of time away from the family. In 1955 she had married Freddie Garland but they divorced a few years later and not long after that she began her relationship with John Houston. As the couple brought up three children – Gary from Cissy's marriage to Garland, along with their own two, Michael and Whitney - life became a juggling act.

Cissy was certainly a shining example of what it meant to combine a successful career with a happy homelife. But that's not to say it was always easy and Whitney said subsequently that she could remember her mother being very concerned about leaving her children, saying "Mommy loves you, but she's got to go to work."

John was willing and able to keep the home fires burning in her absence, but eventually Cissy decided to stop touring and instead focussed on making it as a solo recording artist. She won a contract with Commonwealth United Records and released an album called 'Presenting Cissy Houston' in 1970. Several of the album tracks were released as singles and made the R&B charts including cover versions of *I'll Be There* and *Be My Baby*.

She signed a new deal with Private Stock Records in 1977 and went on to have one of her biggest hits with the title track from her 1978 album *Think It Over*. It was a big disco hit which made # 32 on the Billboard R&B chart in 1979.

Cissy also competed for her country, winning second place for the USA at the World Popular Song Festival that same year with a track called *You're the Fire*, which also appeared on her 1980 album 'Step Aside for a Lady'.

Throughout the 1970s she kept up her session gigs and again worked with leading music artists of the time including Paul Simon, Linda Ronstadt and Kiki Dee. She even sang backing for David Bowie on his 1975 album *Young Americans*.

Later in her career Cissy won a Grammy for Best Traditional Soul Gospel Album for Face to Face (1996). During all the years of her own and Whitney's success, Cissy remained part of the New Hope Baptist Church community and led its 200-strong Youth Inspirational Choir for 50 years.

Her own success notwithstanding, probably Cissy's greatest contribution to the music industry was in creating and guiding the career of her daughter Whitney Houston

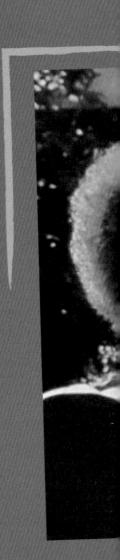

Cissy was the sterner of Whitney's parents, loving but strict. She had high expectations of her children, particularly her daughter. 'Cracking gum or sitting with your legs open were considered unacceptable and I'd better not come back from the yard with scratched knees', Whitney said once when describing her childhood.

For her part, Cissy admitted that she didn't want Whitney dating while she was young. 'I didn't allow it – period,' she said.

Whitney has described her mother as 'my teacher, my friend, the lady in my life', and husband John agreed in subsequent interviews that Cissy taught Whitney everything

Cissy Houston and Whitney (archive footage) in a scene from the promo for the ©Miramax documentary Whitney 2018

As well as sharing her passion for song and introducing Whitney to music through her church, Cissy also taught her daughter all about the music business. As well as showing her singing techniques, Cissy explained all about how to work in a studio and told her more about the negatives of the business, as well as the glory and the glamour.

'I taught her,' says Cissy. 'She sang from the heart. She learned her craft well. She learned the right way because that was what I taught her.

'I taught her that you don't start loud because then you have no place to go. I taught her that songs tell a story, and you don't blare out a story. Control is the basis for singing; up, down, soft, sweet. And diction was very important.'

This note on diction can be heard in the way Whitney finishes off all her words when she's singing – the final t's and ds are never missed or sloppy. The line 'Does he love me, does he love me not' from *How Will I Know* is a great example of this. The final 't' of 'not' is clearly enunciated.

Particularly in the early days of Whitney's career, Cissy was in control and making the decisions. She worked hard to create the career she wanted for her daughter, and particularly in the early days, influenced her choices and the people around her. She provided Whitney with a musical education par excellence.

For her part Whitney never failed to acknowledge her mother's help and support and was keen to involve her when the right opportunities arose. Mother and daughter recorded a studio version of the duet *I Know Him So Well* from the musical *Chess* in 1987 which was included on Whitney's second album, '*Whitney*' and released as the final single from the album in 1989. Cissy also contributed to the soundtrack album for Whitney's hit film *The Preacher's Wife* in 1996.

In 2006, she recorded the song *Family First* with Whitney and Dionne Warwick for the soundtrack to the *Daddy's Little Girls* movie

Following Whitney's death Cissy, who always has strong religious and spiritual beliefs, wrote that: 'when you [Whitney] were born, the Holy Spirit told me you would not be with me long and I thank God for the beautiful flower he allowed me to raise and cherish for 48 years'

When you believe

As a teenager, Whitney had begun to see for herself that not everyone had the same opportunities in life. She was determined to make the most of any chances that came her way and decided to become a professional singer when she was just 13.

She was very much in touch with her spirituality and went to church regularly for services, bible readings and choir practice.

Whitney was a shy and unassuming child and didn't really have many friends outside of the church. As she explained to *Time* magazine; 'In grammar school some of the girls had problems with me. My face was too light. My hair was too long. It was the black-consciousness period, and I felt really bad. I finally faced the fact that it isn't a crime not having friends. Being alone means you have fewer problems. When I decided to be a singer, my mother warned me I'd be alone a lot. Basically, we all are. Loneliness comes with life.'

So for a long time none of her schoolmates were aware of Whitney's talents. Notwithstanding the fact that she didn't ever perform there, Whitney's former grammar school in East Orange, NJ, was renamed The Whitney E. Houston Academy For Creative And Performing Arts in 1997. Whitney and her husband Bobby Brown attended the ceremony.

However as a teenager Whitney did make a very close friend in Robyn Crawford, a schoolmate a few years her senior, who she had met through her older brothers. Their friendship would be enduring and strong. Robyn would look out for Whitney – a role she continued throughout their adult life. She was Whitney's closest confidante and went on to work in her professional team as her assistant and creative director.

Throughout their time together, rumours surrounding their friendship persisted, with several commentators speculating that the pair were in a romantic relationship. While Whitney would always deny such talk, Robyn did address the subject in a 2019 interview with BBC music reporter Mark Savage to publicise her memoir, '*A Song For You*'.

Whitney photographed in February 1982 when she was a senior in high school

'In grammar school some of the girls had problems with me...'

'We met, we clicked and we became friends', said Robyn. 'We built that friendship on being open and honest with each other about everything. She told me she was going to sign this [record] deal and she was going to take me with her all around the world. And along the way, we had an intimate, loving, physical experience of friendship *within* our friendship. It was love and it was open and honest.'

Robyn said that Whitney ended the relationship because of the record deal, telling her, it would make our journey even more difficult.

'Whitney shared with me her belief that, if people found out about our relationship, they would use it against us,' said Robyn. 'And it was the 80s. You were either this or that. And women were treated in a way where they were rivals and not comrades. So it was a lot and we were young. We were young, but we were fearless.

'Whitney said "I want you right here. You know me. You knew me before we got where we were going." So we were a team. She knew me and she trusted me.'

Their friendship was solid enough to withstand any hiccups and continued for many years.

Other reviews of Whitney's life include mention of a time of teenage rebellion – possibly linked to the fact that her parents separated in 1977 when Whitney was 15. However, John only moved 10 minutes away from the family home and still played a big part in Whitney's life. Her parents did not divorce until 1991.

The 'rebellion' was mostly small scale, involving staying out late and slacking on household chores – but as Cissy described things; 'She was lazier than hell, stubborn and opinionated. When she was 16, I told her she wasn't going to make 17 because I was gonna kill her'.

Throughout her youth singing Gospel remained Whitney's passion and gave her energy. She sang from the heart and learned her craft well, with her mother Cissy as her teacher.

Eventually Whitney felt ready to sing outside of church and began to join her mother on stage sometimes, as a backing singer, and including a period while Cissy was promoting *Think It Over* in the late 1970s. From a very young age Whitney had often accompanied Cissy to work in countless recording studios so it was a fairly seamless transition from watching to participating.

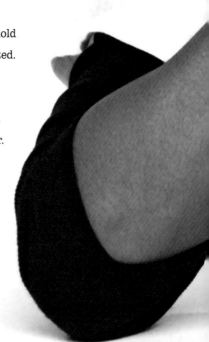

Whitney photographed in February 1982 when she was a senior in high school

'I remember when I was six or seven, crawling up to the window to watch my mother sing', Whitney recalled. 'And I'd be talking to "Aunt Ree". I had no idea that Aretha Franklin was famous, just that I like to hear her sing too!'

Whitney credits Aretha as one of her greatest inspirations, after her mother and her family. 'I was in the studios and I saw Aretha and Sweet Inspirations. And I heard Aretha's voice ... and I said if I could ever be a singer that's the way I wanted to make people feel.'

So aged around 14 Whitney started singing with her mother on stage in clubs and began to hone her craft. But she also had talents in other directions and a few years later she was scouted by a local modelling agency called Click Models. She won plenty of work, usually for editorial spreads in magazines such as *Seventeen* and *Cosmopolitan*. She also did a little acting, mainly in sitcoms. Concert promoters Eugene Harvey and Seymour Flics began managing Whitney in 1981 and decided that developing modelling and acting would work well for her.

But, while Whitney enjoyed the work and its rewards, she knew in her heart she wanted to sing. She got a big chance when she joined her mother backing Chaka Khan on a few tracks for her album *Naughty'; Clouds* and *Our Love's in Danger*.

Then Whitney got her first opportunity to work as a featured vocalist in 1982 when she was 19. It was on the ballad called *Memories* for experimental jazz-funk ensemble called Material and their album *One Down*. The trio, comprising bass player Bill Laswell, keyboard player Martin Beinhorn and sound engineer Martin Bisi never performed their own vocals and instead employed a variety of singers. The *Village Voice* magazine review of the album mentioned Whitney's track in particular, describing it as 'gorgeous'.

This and other opportunities, such as appearances in her mother's shows, were coming together so that Whitney was beginning to attract attention. Other early press mentions include one from *Billboard* which included, presciently, the thought that; 'Whitney has the pedigree and the style to be a major vocalist.'

Since signing with the personal management company in 1981, Whitney had attracted offers from major record labels. But her canny management team, backed by Cissy, were determined not to rush into anything nor to put pressure on young Whitney herself.

But eventually the right deal came around. Enter Clive Davis, president and founder of Arista Records. He was determined to make Whitney a star.

Whitney in a photography fashion session in New York City in September of 1980

'Whitney has the pedigree and the style to be a major vocalist.'

Breaking through (1984-85)

As soon as Arista president Clive Davis heard Whitney singing at a nightclub he knew she was what he'd been looking for. He had long held a vision of creating a pop icon with mass appeal, rather than create another successful artist in the more niche area of R&B – well respected though that was.

He wanted to create a 'Barbra Streisand of pop' – and considered Whitney to be the talented but blank canvas he could use to create a mega star. 'I was stunned by her talent," he said. "I wanted to sign her immediately.'

He was quick to offer her a recording contract – and Whitney and her team were equally quick to accept. Cissy knew that Clive was a respected and talented executive. Since founding Arista in 1974 he had enjoyed success after success with artists such as Barry Manilow, Patti Smith, Ray Parker Jr. and Melissa Manchester.

Very relevantly to the Houston family he had also revived the careers of Dionne Warwick and Aretha Franklin.

Clive was in no hurry to push Whitney, who at that time was still a diamond in the rough. He knew she needed polish and confidence and was prepared to put in the work to get her to where he knew she could be – right at the top of the industry. He spent a full two years developing Whitney – perfecting her image, choosing her songs, finessing her sound – and began showcasing her before she ever released an album through guest appearances on chat shows and at industry events and parties.

Her first single was a 1984 duet with former Harold Melvin and the Blue Notes vocalist Teddy Pendergrass on his album *Love Language*. Their track, *Hold Me*, missed the Top 40 of the Billboard Hot 100, but reached number five on the R&B chart.

Then in February 1985 came the release of her debut album *Whitney Houston*. Clive Davis had planned to invest US$250,000 on developing and recording this first album – an unprecedented investment in a debut album at the time – but eventually spent even more, an estimated $US 400,000. It wasn't all plain sailing either – some producers weren't willing to risk working on a pop album with an unknown gospel singer.

Whitney at The Poplar Creek Music Theater In Hoffman Estates, Illinois, June 25, 1985

However things began to fall into place when fellow Arista signing, songwriter-producer Kashif Saleem, agreed to produce the album's opening track, *You Give Good Love* and the second track *Thinking About You*, on which he also duetted with Whitney.

Then Arista's A&R supremo Gerry Griffith got in touch with Narada Michael Walden, already on his way to becoming the hit record producer, songwriter, artist he is today, and persuaded him to come on board.

Speaking to *Songwriter Universe* magazine Walden explained how he came to co-write and produce *How Will I Know* '[Gerry] said, "You've gotta make time [to work with Whitney Houston]. Let me send you this idea for a song that we're thinking about for you." So I get the song and hear it, and I said, "This song isn't complete—it doesn't have any verse." So I told Gerry that he's got to call the writers and ask them if I could write a verse, because there's no verse in the song. And they said, "Okay, let's see what you want to do." So then I banged it out with the whole band—the same band I'd been working with for Aretha's album... I sing the whole melody and [tell them] how I wanted it to go. And they said, "We want to put our own lyric," and I said, "no problem." So they put their lyric in.

We then cut it and I called Whitney. I said, "I want to work with you on this song, but I don't want to cut it in too high a key," because the [opening verse melody] already starts high. She said, "No, I like it—go ahead and cut it high." At the time Whitney was a new artist—I didn't know yet how great her range was. But when I got to New York (to record her vocals), there she was in the studio, looking laid-back and confident, and looking gorgeous. Then she goes to the mic, and she just floors me! She sang it just like you hear on the record—the whole thing. She's incredible. And then, since I knew her mother (Cissy Houston) and had worked with her, I asked Whitney to call her mother, to come to the studio and bring some of her friends (who were singers), to sing background vocals. They did, and Whitney, Cissy and the two other singers sang the backgrounds great and it was done.'

Walden went on to produce more hits for Whitney than any other producer.

The other key figure on the album was Jermaine Jackson, older brother of Michael, who had signed with Arista in 1984. He produced three songs, *Someone For Me,* and *Nobody Loves Me Like You Do* and *Take Good Care of My Heart*, on which he also duets.

Then came some magic from Michael Masser, a successful songwriter and producer who had already had massive success with Diana Ross and her hits 'Touch Me In The Morning' and *Theme from Mahogany (Do You Know Where You're Going To)*. Michael had met Whitney a few years earlier when he was producing the Teddy Pendergrass album, featuring her track *Hold Me*. This time Whitney was centre stage and Michael came on board to handle the 'pop' side of her album. The combination of her vocals and Michael's writing and production talents was perfection on four of the album tracks, including *The Greatest Love of All* and *Saving All My Love*.

Whitney performing in Los Angeles, circa 1985

The album started slowly – but was a grower. The music was boosted by a phenomenal marketing campaign around Whitney by Arista, beginning with a much-coveted appearance on *The Merv Griffin Show,* followed by other star-studded performance 'showcases' on the east and west coasts of America. There was also a hugely successful push to gain editorial coverage in newspapers and magazines, creating a massive buzz around this formerly unknown model and gospel singer.

The first single release was *Someone for Me*, which didn't make much impact. But the second release, *You Give Good Love*, provided 22-year-old Whitney with her first hit, topping the R&B chart and making #3 on the Billboard Hot 100.

Then Whitney announced her arrival as a top music artist emphatically as her next three singles became massive hits. *Saving All My Love for You*, *How Will I Know*, and *The Greatest Love of All* sold in their millions, and all made #1 in the charts. *Whitney Houston* became both the first debut album and the first album by a female solo artist to produce three #1 singles.

Within the year the album itself was #1 on the Billboard 200, a position it held for 14 weeks, selling over 13 million copies in America alone, making it the best-selling debut ever by a female artist. Eventually *Whitney Houston* was certified 13 times platinum by the Recording Industry Association of America (RIAA) and achieved global sales of 22 million copies, making it one of the best-selling albums of all time. Clive's investment turned out to be money well spent. Miss Whitney Houston was a star.

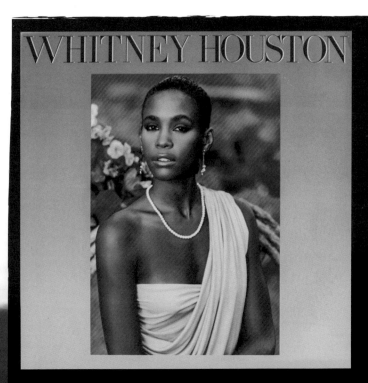

Whitney Houston

**Whitney's self-titled debut album
Released in February 1985 by Arista Records**

Track list

- You Give Good Love
- Thinking About You
- Someone For Me
- Saving All My Love for You
- Nobody Loves Me Like You Do
- How Will I Know
- All At Once
- Take Good Care of My Heart
- Greatest Love of All
- Hold Me (with Teddy Pendergrass)

Whitney June 1985

Clive Davis

Legendary record label executive Clive Davis was born in Brooklyn, New York, in 1932.

After graduating from New York University and Harvard Law School, he practiced law before beginning his career in the music business with Columbia Records. He became company president in 1967 and was responsible for signing major artists including Chicago, Santana, Billy Joel, Bruce Springsteen, Neil Diamond, Pink Floyd, and The Isley Brothers. He was also key in the careers of Barbra Streisand, Bob Dylan, Andy Williams and Simon and Garfunkel.

After leaving Columbia in 1973, he co-founded Arista Records the following year. The company got off to an incredible start when Barry Manilow's hit song *Mandy*, which Clive had found and named, went to #1.

As well as launching the careers of Barry Manilow and Whitney Houston, Clive and Arista worked with a roster of big music stars including The Grateful Dead, The Kinks, Lou Reed, Eurythmics, Daryl Hall and John Oates, and Carly Simon.

Clive was also important to Dionne Warwick and Aretha Franklin. Dionne's career, which had stalled in the 1970s, was revived when she moved to Arista in 1979 and she enjoyed another slew of hit records through to the late 1980s.

Similarly, Aretha was courted by Clive after a dry spell in the mid-70s and joined Arista in 1979, remaining with the label for 23 years. Her Arista hits include *Who's Zoomin Who* and *Jump*.

More recently, in 2000, Clive formed the J Records label and again had immediate success, this time with Alicia Keys debut album *Songs In A Minor* and its follow up *The Diary of Alicia Keys*. J Records has since had successes with Maroon 5, Annie Lennox and Luther Vandross. Clive also worked with Rod Stewart on his career-reviving five albums in *The Great American Songbook* series.

As a producer he has won a total of five Grammy awards and was inducted into the Rock and Roll Hall of Fame as a non-performer in 2000.

And of course, it was under his guidance that Whitney Houston became one of the biggest-selling artists in music history.

Music executive Clive Davis introduces Whitney Houston in 1984 in New York

Stevie Wonder, Babyface, Whitney Houston, LA Reid, Narada Michael Walden and Clive Davis attend a party circa 1988

Breaking records (1986-89)

At the start of 1986 Whitney's name was on the lips of fans and industry professionals alike and the awards and accolades began rolling in.

Billboard magazine named her its number one 'Top New Pop Artist' and 'Top New Black Artist' and she won two American Music Awards – with *Saving All My Love For You* winning the category of Favourite Video/Single and *You Give Good Love* as Favourite Single, Soul/R&B. *Rolling Stone* magazine's annual readers' poll ranked Whitney as Best New Female Singer.

Most pleasingly of all for Whitney, she won that year's prestigious Grammy award for Best Pop Vocal Performance – Female, for *Saving All My Love for You*, a song she also sang live during the ceremony.

Whitney beat a strong category of fellow nominees including Madonna and Tina Turner and was particularly delighted that coincidentally the award was presented by her cousin Dionne Warwick. Announcing Whitney as the winner, Dionne couldn't hide her excitement, jumping up and down after she'd opened the envelope. Once Whitney got on stage the two cousins hugged and cried happy tears, as Cissy watched on, clapping in the audience.

'Can you believe this!' said Whitney as she began her acceptance speech. 'Oh my goodness. First I give thanks to God who makes it all possible for me'. She also thanked her parents, 'The two most important people in my life' and Dionne and Clive Davis among others.

Now a worldwide phenomenon, Whitney needed a team around her and naturally looked to her family for support and expertise.

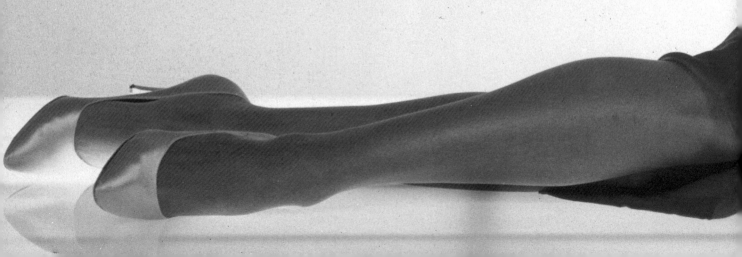

Portrait of Whitney, 1987

While Clive Davis masterminded Whitney's career, looking after her artistic interests, her father John was put in charge of the business side. John used his experience managing The Gospelaires and Sweet Inspirations in the 1960s to become his daughter's business manager and Chief Executive Officer of her company, Nippy Incorporated.

As he told *Ebony* magazine in 1990; 'I am smart, I learn fast and I'm dedicated to Whitney Houston. It is her career, her money and nobody makes decisions but her... I come across to some people as the devil incarnate.'

Whitney was happy to have her father at the helm of her new empire. 'I figured that if there is anybody I can trust, it is my daddy, because I know my daddy loves me. And I know that before the business and the money came, it was just him and family...And besides that fact, my father has a good business mind' she said in her own separate interview with *Ebony* at that time.

'I just feel comfortable with him being there. I feel secure that somebody is watching over me and watching over everybody else too. I trust him. He literally came in and saw the troubled areas and what needed to be done, what I needed to do, and we did it.'

Her utter and solid belief in her father in those early days makes their eventual fall out all the sadder. But for now, things were good.

Cissy was still heavily involved in Whitney's life, professionally and personally, and brothers Gary and Michael worked for her as well, on the singing and management side respectively. Whitney was now a rich woman, so she bought her own apartment, close to her family home, and splashed out on a new car, a Mercedes. But other than that, she spoke of wanting to take things slowly; 'My mother always told me, before the fall goeth pride... I've been enjoying this business longer than people think, and much longer than the public has known me. Longevity is what counts in this business.'

Like many supposed 'overnight sensations', Whitney had of course put the work in for many years and been singing professionally for eight. So while fame and travel was new to her, actual 'showbusiness' was not and her time as a model meant she was used to being stared at. 'From the beginning the camera and I were great friends,' she said. 'I know the eye of the camera is on me – eye to eye. It loves me, and I love it.'

She appeared to be handling all the attention well and was determined to pace herself by carving out personal time and space in her schedule. 'I need private time' she told interviewers even at that early stage of her career.

Whitney live on stage at Wembley Arena, London, during the Greatest Love World Tour in October 1986

In October 1986 Whitney made her first trip to the UK for three concerts at Wembley Arena in London and one night in Scotland as part of her four-month long debut world tour. Titled *The Greatest Love World Tour*, it took in Europe, Japan and Australia, as well as dates all over the US. Right after the tour, Whitney embarked on a series of recording sessions for her second album. Again Clive Davis paid incredible attention to detail, and it was a long time in planning and development. Titled *Whitney* – such was her fame that she no longer needed to use her surname – it was a pacier affair, using many of the producers from the first album.

Released in June 1987, *Whitney* flew straight into the charts at #1 on the Billboard 200 – making it the first album by a female artist to do so. It included four tracks which would be number one singles and long-lasting hits; *I Wanna Dance with Somebody (Who Loves Me)*, *Didn't We Almost Have It All, So Emotional* and *Where Do Broken Hearts Go*.

The success of these four singles combined with the three from her debut album to give Whitney the unprecedented achievement of having seven consecutive #1 hits by any performer. *Whitney* was also certified diamond by RIAA and topped charts around the world. It stayed at #1 in the US for a record-breaking 11 consecutive weeks.

Whitney's second album
Released in June 1987 by Arista Records

Track list

- **I Wanna Dance with Somebody (Who Loves me)**
- **Just The Lonely Talking Again**
- **Love Will Save The Day**
- **Didn't We Almost Have It All**
- **So Emotional**
- **Where You Are**
- **Love is a Contact Sport**
- **You're Still My Man**
- **For The Love of You**
- **Where Do Broken Hearts Go**
- **I Know Him So Well (from Chess)**

Whitney performs at the Nelson Mandela Freedom
Festival at Clapham Common in London, 1986

the 1988 Grammy Awards *Whitney* received three nominations, including for Album of the Year and won Best Pop Vocal Performance, Female, for *I Wanna Dance with Somebody (Who Loves Me)*. With sales of over 20 million copies, the album remains one of the best-sellers of all time. Whitney's superstar status was cemented with this second album.

Her talent and professionalism was second to none. Her bodyguard at the time, David Roberts would spend months at a time with her on tour and marvelled at her command of her work. He said he once witnessed her walk into a recording studio, perform a single take of *One Moment in Time* for the 1988 Olympic Games, and leave 20 minutes later having delivered a note-perfect rendition. 'She was known as "One-take Houston",' he said. 'She was back before the hamburgers got cold.'

The tour to support the album was titled *The Moment of Truth World Tour* and ran from July 1987 until November 1988, taking in the US, UK, Europe, Australia and Asia.

In Europe, Whitney visited a total of 12 countries, playing to over half a million fans, including nine sold out dates at Wembley Arena in London. While in the UK Whitney also headlined a gala celebration in honour of Nelson Mandela's 70th birthday.

Tour over and Whitney was back home in the US, where she performed at the 1989 Soul Train Awards on April 13. It was a significant night; chiefly because she met rap star Bobby Brown - the man who was to become her husband and the father of her only child.

Record-breaking singles success

Whitney's seven consecutive hits on the American Billboard Hot 100 chart were:

- *Saving All My Love for You* - for three weeks in October 1985
- *How Will I Know* - one week in February 1986,
- *Greatest Love of All* - five weeks in May 1986
- *I Wanna Dance with Somebody (Who Loves Me)* - three weeks in July 1987
- *Didn't We Almost Have It All* - three weeks in September 1987
- *So Emotional* – one week in October 1987
- *Where Do Broken Hearts Go* - three weeks in April 1988

Whitney on Stage, 1987

At the time Bobby Brown was about as famous as he was going to get. The 'bad boy of rap' had a huge hit with his *Don't Be Cruel* R&B album which had given him five Top 10 hit singles including *My Prerogative* and *Every Little Step*.

He had a high-powered, sexually charged performance style which earned him comparisons with his childhood hero Michael Jackson. In a later interview with *Rolling Stone* magazine, Whitney said; 'He was hot, he was on fire ... I and some friends of mine were sitting behind him. I was hugging them, we were laughing and I kept hitting Bobby in the back of the head. I leaned over and said "Bobby, I'm so sorry" and he turned around and looked at me, like, "Yeah, well just don't let it happen again". And I was like "Oooh this guy doesn't like me". Well, I always get curious when somebody doesn't like me'.

Bobby was six years her junior, but already had three children by two women. As well as his reputation as a womaniser, Bobby was known to have been involved with gangs and guns. His 'bad boy' image intrigued Whitney – so she invited him to her 26th birthday party that August and they danced together all evening.

The pair were a prime example of opposites attracting - he was street and had swag, whereas she had a squeaky-clean image and sang about love. Although on paper it was a mismatch, they had an incredible chemistry. The stage was set for a relationship of complexity, of highs and lows, rows and make ups, all flavoured with alcohol and drugs. Many of those close to Whitney at the time, attribute to the change in her to the start of her relationship with Bobby.

Whitney performs on stage at Wembley Arena, London, 15th May 1988

'He was hot, he was on fire ...'

Whitney is ushered by a bodyguard through a frenzied crowd of fans at Kai Tak Airport. She is going to hold three concerts at the Hong Kong Coliseum, 1988

Finding her way (1990-92)

No album selling 10 million copies worldwide and going four times platinum could be described as a disappointment, but when your first two albums sold around twice that there would be cause for concern. That was what happened to Whitney with her third album release, *I'm Your Baby Tonight*.

Released in November 1990, *I'm Your Baby Tonight* was quite different from her first two album releases, being more R&B orientated. Clive Davis had executive produced and Narada Michael Walden and Michael Masser were also producers. Additions to the team were R&B hitmakers L.A. Reid and Babyface, and Whitney also included collaborations with Luther Vandross and Stevie Wonder.

Whitney herself also had more input into this album. Of course, by this time she was a more confident woman and artist with experience and opinions of her own, so a desire for more involvement was natural enough. But Whitney was also mindful that the charts were changing and now ruled by rappers, R&B, hip hop and new jack swing stars.

Whitney herself had faced accusations of selling out on black music and was upset that she had been booed at the Soul Train Awards for two years running in 1988 and 1989. In contrast to the cheers for other nominees, there had been jeers from the audience in 1988 when Whitney's name was read out as a nominee in both the Best Music Video and Best R&B Urban Contemporary Single by a Female – and she won neither award. Then the following year she again received boos when her name was read out as a nominee for Best R&B/Urban Contemporary Single –Female, and again she did not win.

Commentators at the time decided that black audiences weren't happy with her 'mainstream, white-friendly' image and 'middle of the road' pop output. There was a new mood of self-awareness among America's black population and music fans wanted to celebrate their own culture and sound.

Whitney said later that she found the incident difficult. 'It's not a good feeling. It's kind of funny though. You think, are they booing me? They are. Then you have to sit there and be cordial and smiley, like everything is ok.'

Whitney charms the press, 1990

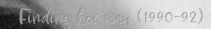

'It's not a good feeling. It's kind of funny though. You think, are they booing me?...'

Whitney and Bobby Brown, 1992

Whitney and Clive Davis at an AIDS benefit, 1990

Dionne Warwick & Whitney perform together, 1990

I'm Your Baby Tonight

**Whitney's third album
Released in November 1990 by Arista Records**

Track list

- I'm Your Baby Tonight
- My Name Is Not Susan
- All The Man That I Need
- Lover for Life
- Anymore
- Miracle
- I Belong To You
- Who Do You Love
- We Didn't Know (with Stevie Wonder)
- After We Make Love
- I'm Knockin'

From the start Clive Davis and Arista had marketed Whitney as a mainstream pop star, with little consideration of the changing expectations among her original black community. Throughout her career she was somehow considered 'not black enough' which is a mystery to many commentators when you compare her to other black stars who were similarly into more mainstream music.

In his 2013 memoir *The Soundtrack of My Life*, Clive Davis concedes that he perhaps missed a trick here. 'Frankly, I was color-blind, and perhaps a little naïve in that I didn't try to find pure R&B songs that only black-oriented stations could claim for their own,' he said.

'For Whitney's third album it was clear that we needed to shore up her base in the black community. This was not a response to what happened at the Soul Train Awards or to any of the other criticisms of her, which Whitney and I never discussed. It just seemed the next logical step in her growth and progression as an artist. Up until this time our goal had purely and simply been to find the best songs for her'.

Reflecting on the booing episodes, Whitney said, 'Sometimes it gets down to, You're not black enough for them. You're not R&B enough. You're very pop. The white audience has taken you away from them.' Although she had appeared to take the snub in her stride, according to those close to her at the time she was emotionally devastated. The saxophonist in her band, Kirk Whalum, said he felt she never recovered from it. 'That was one of the boxes that were ticked from which she eventually perished', he said in Nick Broomfield's documentary, *Whitney: Can I Be Me*.

However, at the time, the incident didn't seem to rain on her parade. After all she had already won 11 American Music Awards and two Grammys, achieved the biggest-selling debut album by a female artist in history and clocked up her record-breaking run of seven consecutive No 1 singles in America.

I'm Your Baby Tonight made its debut at #22 on the Billboard 200 chart, rising to #5 and then peaking at #3 and remaining in the top 10 for 22 weeks and in the chart for a week short of a year.

It made #1 in the Billboard Top R&B Albums chart and was also the year end #1 album on that chart for 1991. The album was also an international hit, including in the UK where it got to it #4.

Two other tracks from the album were #1 singles in the US – the title track, *I'm Your Baby Tonight* and *All The Man That I Need*.

'I'm Your Baby Tonight' World Tour, May 16 1991 at the Great Western Forum in Inglewood, California

However, some reviewers thought the material was generally of a lesser quality than her previous albums and, overall, sales were fewer and tapered off more quickly.

Nevertheless, Whitney remained popular. She was chosen to sing the US national anthem at the 1992 Superbowl XXV in February 1991 and her outstanding performance was recorded and released as a charity single which became the highest-ever charting rendition of the anthem on the Billboard Hot 100. All proceeds, a combined contribution of US$531,650, from the Whitney Houston Foundation for Children, Inc., Arista and Bertelsmann Music Group Distribution (BMG), went to charity to the American Red Cross Gulf Crisis Fund in aid of US military personnel, their family and war victims in the region.

Whitney described her performance in a later interview, saying; 'If you were there, you could feel the intensity. You know, we were in the Gulf War at the time. It was an intense time for our country. A lot of our daughters and sons were overseas fighting. I could see... in the stadium...I could see the fear, the hope, the intensity, the prayers going up, you know, and I just felt like this is the moment. And it was hope, we needed hope, you know, to bring our babies home and that's what it was about for me, that what I felt when I sang that song, and the overwhelming love coming out of the stands was incredible.'

Her recording was re-released in 2001 following the 9/11 terrorist attacks to raise money for the firefighters and victims. This time the single made it to number six on the Billboard Hot 100 chart, giving Whitney her last top 10 hit during her lifetime and making her the first artist to take the anthem into the Top 10.

From March to October 1991 Whitney travelled the world with her *I'm Your Baby Tonight* tour, taking in almost 100 dates in North America and Europe, including 10 nights in London, six nights in Birmingham and three nights in Glasgow in the UK. Speaking in the 2017 Whitney documentary *'Can I Be Me'* her saxophonist Kirk Whalum said; 'There were moments when we and the audience were transformed by her voice and that's a God thing, that's not a human thing. Whitney had a gift – she could knock us over with a gospel riff. She could caress a note.'

She delighted audiences with her performances. And all was well outside of work as her relationship with Bobby Brown was going strong. Things were looking good.

Whitney sings the National Anthem during the pregame show at Super Bowl XXV, Jan 27 1991

If you were there, you could feel the intensity...

Kevin Costner & Whitney in The BodyGuard, 1992

The Bodyguard

In 1992, at the height of her fame as a singer, Whitney undertook her first major movie role, starring in the musical film The Bodyguard, alongside Kevin Costner.

The script for the romantic drama had been around for years and centred around a bodyguard who reluctantly signs up to protect a superstar singer, something of a diva, who is receiving threatening letters. At one time was mooted as a vehicle for Diana Ross. Then in the early 1990s Kevin Costner got involved and, riding on the back of his success in the films *Dances With Wolves*, *JFK* and *Robin Hood: Prince of Thieves*, he became heavily involved in the film's development.

It was Costner who wanted Whitney for the role and actually delayed production for a year while he waited for her to finish her *I'm Your Baby Tonight* world tour and sign up. He decided that she was perfect for the part of lead character Rachel Marron but had his work cut out both in persuading Whitney to take the part and the Warner Brothers studio to accept her.

Whitney wasn't easy to convince. Although she was interested in reigniting her teenage acting career, she had envisaged making her debut in a smaller role and was fearful of taking a lead part.

Similarly, the studio had a lot riding on the film and, feeling uneasy about her lack of acting experience, asked her to take a screen test.

'She had to earn the role', Costner said afterwards. Then speaking in his eulogy at Whitney's funeral he expanded on his thoughts, saying; 'The Whitney I knew, despite her success and worldwide fame, still wondered: Am I good enough? Am I pretty enough? Will they like me?

It was the burden that made her great

'Whitney if you could hear me now I would tell you, you weren't just good enough — you were great. You sang the whole damn song without a band. You made the picture what it was.

'A lot of leading men could have played my part, a lot of guys could have filled that role, but you, Whitney, I truly believed that you were the only one who that could have played Rachel Marron at that time.'

Eventually bearing out Kevin Costner's belief in the film and in Whitney, *The Bodyguard* went on to become a huge hit at the box office.

Although the film had its critics (it is listed in The Official Razzie Movie Guide as one of The 100 'Most Enjoyably Bad Movies Ever Made') it was a hit with the public and did great at the box office. In the US, where it opened on the same day as Disney's *Aladdin* on 25 November 1992, it was the third best performing film that week, grossing US$16.6 million in its opening weekend. The film spent 10 weeks in the Top 10, ultimately grossing $121.9 million domestically, and $410.9 million worldwide.

In the UK, it had a record Christmas opening, with a gross of $2 million for the weekend. It was the seventh highest-grossing film of 1992 in the United States and Canada and the second highest-grossing film of 1992, worldwide, behind *Aladdin*. At the time, it was the tenth highest-grossing film of all time.

It grossed more than $410 million and when it was re-released in 2012 it grossed a further $61,020.

Then the soundtrack took off on a staggeringly successful journey of its own – to this day it is the best-selling movie soundtrack of all time, with sales of an incredible 45 million copies around the world – and of course spawning the huge hit *I Will Always Love You*.

This song is a cover of Dolly Parton's 1974 ballad, reinterpreted by Whitney to stunning effect. She begins the song singling a capella, which was apparently Kevin Costner's idea, then builds to a climax of incredible vocal acrobatics. It was the right voice, the right song and the right time and stayed at #1 on the Billboard Hot 100 for 14 weeks. It also spent 10 weeks in the UK charts, the longest run by any female artist at that time.

Whitney co-executive produced and recorded six songs for the soundtrack which earned her three Grammy Awards, including Album of the Year and Record of the Year.

It won three Grammy's and included other hits including Queen of the Night, I Have Nothing and Run to You.

Whitney dressed to impress in The BodyGuard, 1992

Whitney in a still from the The BodyGuard, 1992

The Bodyguard

Soundtrack album
Released in November 1992 by Arista Records.

Track list

- I Will Always Love You
- I Have Nothing
- I'm Every Woman
- Run To You
- Queen Of The Night
- Jesus Loves Me
- Even If My Heart Would Break

- Someday (I'm Coming Back)
- It's Gonna Be A Lovely Day
- What's So Funny 'Bout Peace, Love and Understanding
- Theme from The Bodyguard
- Trust In Me

Didn't we almost have it all?

Three years after their first meeting, Whitney married Bobby on 18 July 1992. This 'celebrity wedding of the year' was a private ceremony at Whitney's $10 million mansion in New Jersey.

Whitney wore a full-length white fitted beaded lace wedding dress with matching headpiece and was attended by her friend Robyn Crawford as maid of honour, and bridesmaids including singers CeCe Winans and Pebbles.

Cameras were kept away as Whitney and Bobby welcomed a star-studded guest list including Dionne Warwick, Patti LaBelle and actor Kevin Costner, her co-star in The Bodyguard.

Although many of their friends and family couldn't see the relationship lasting, Whitney seemed convinced they were a good match.

'You know, Bobby and I basically come from the same place,' she told *Rolling Stone* magazine. 'Bobby comes from Boston, out of the projects. I come from Newark, out of the projects. Bobby has two very strong parents; I have two very strong parents.'

In a February 1992 profile of the couple in *Vanity Fair*, writer Lynn Hirschberg described them as the "inverse of Fred Astaire and Ginger Rogers. Like Ginger, Bobby gives a sexual charge to the pure image of Whitney (Fred), while she graces him with a veneer of class."

During their first year of marriage things seemed to go well and the couple welcomed their first and only child, a daughter named Bobbi Kristina Brown, on 4 March 1993. But before too long things began to go wrong and rumours swirled around the couple, including the long-running speculation about a love affair between Whitney and her friend Robyn Crawford. Bobby faced continued accusations of infidelity.

As well as managing the press speculation, Whitney was dealing with the same difficulties her own mother had faced in trying to combine a successful and demanding career with motherhood. Whitney had described the birth of Bobbi Kristina as the most 'incredible' moment in her life.

Bobby Brown and Whitney circa 1994

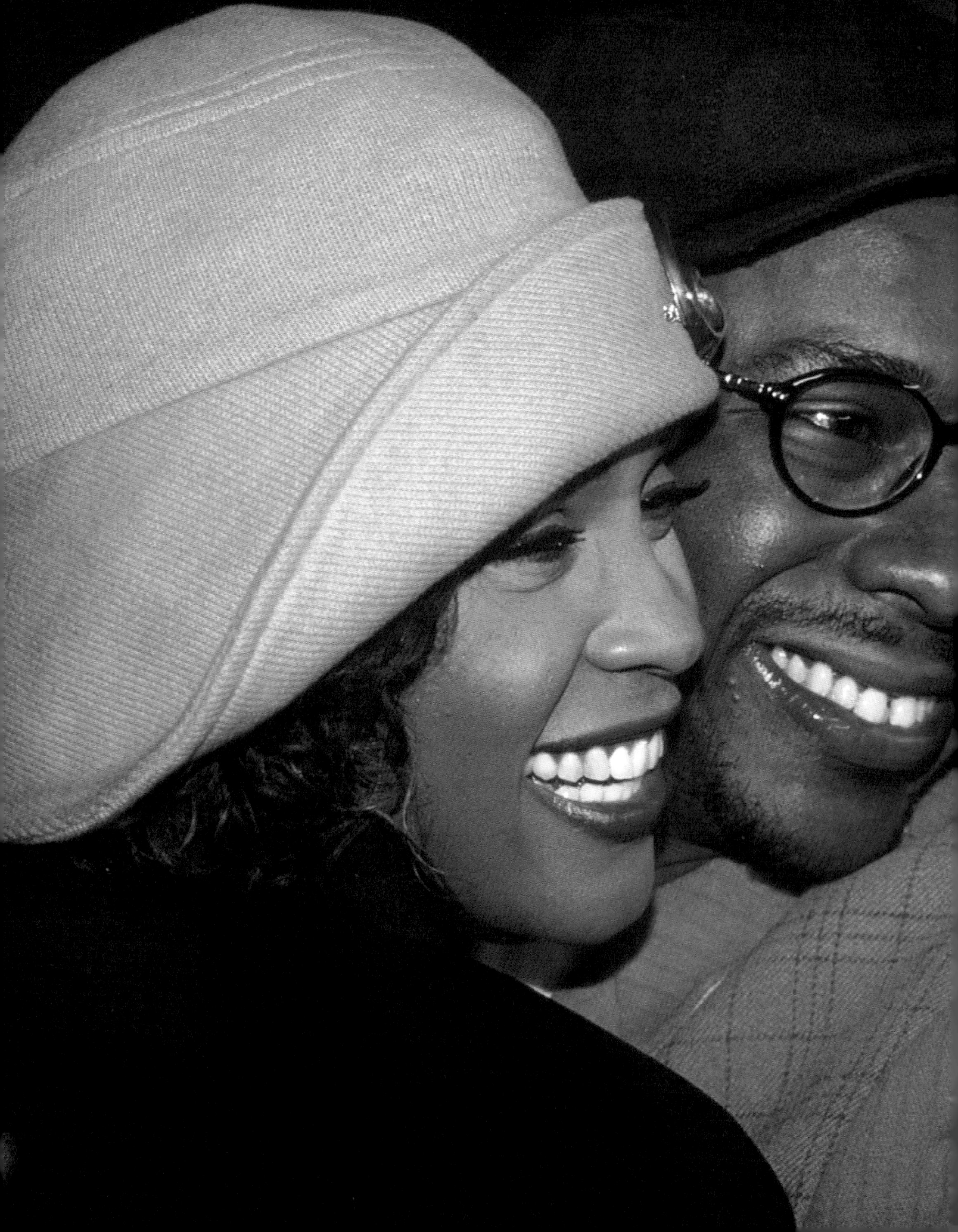

'God knows, I have been in front of millions and millions of people, and that has been incredible, to feel that give-take thing,' Whitney told *Rolling Stone* magazine. 'But man, when I gave birth to her and they put her in my arms, I thought: "This has got to be it. This is the ultimate." I haven't experienced anything greater.'

But Whitney's international career meant that she had to spend weeks apart from her young daughter.

Whenever it was possible, Whitney would bring Bobbi Kristina with her to concerts and mother and daughter would share the stage for a song or two. Fans loved it but were unaware that behind-the-scenes things were rather unsettled. Bobby was also often away on tour and promoting his music.

According to Whitney's bodyguard at the time, David Roberts who worked for her from 1988 until 1995, all was not well at home. He put many of the family's problems down to the fact that while both Bobby and Whitney maintained successful careers during the early days of the marriage, Bobby ultimately played second fiddle to his wife whose career skyrocketed following the success of *The Bodyguard*. Whitney was riding high professionally, particularly as she won award after award for *I Will Always Love You* and *The Bodyguard Soundtrack* album, including American Music Awards, a Brit award and three Grammys.

And although Bobby was also still successful, he was undoubtedly in a lower league than his wife. According to David Roberts, Bobby '... lost his own identity, which I suspect he resented deeply, especially as his own talents were inferior to Miss Houston's. It was a pervasive atmosphere. In the days prior to the advent of Mr Brown, we'd go shopping to a mall, we could buy some clothes, get a cup of coffee. However, when we tried the same in the presence of 'Mr Whitney Houston', then it became a complete battle as to who could attract the most attention; and the more he tried it, the more she tried to meet it.

'That was her problem all the way along – whatever he did, she tried to do the same to make him feel comfortable in an environment where he was otherwise totally out of his depth.

'[Brown] was jealous of her success, so he rubbed her face in his cheating, but she forgave him every possible indiscretion. I just couldn't understand it. And it ate away at her.'

Bobby Brown and Whitney attend the 'Cinderella' movie premiere at the Sony Lincoln Square Theater in New York City on October 27, 1997

Both Whitney and Bobby sought to make things better with drugs and alcohol. Bobby faced a couple of drug and drink-driving charges during their marriage and Whitney later admitted that her personal drug use became 'heavy' after *The Bodyguard* was released and that by 1996 she was using drugs every day. Several documentaries on Whitney suggest she had nurtured a recreational drugs habit since her teens and her brother Michael is on record as saying the same. But in the Nineties her drug use increased dramatically.

David Roberts described Bobbi Kristina as being 'born into chaos. I watched Bobbi Kristina as a little girl, running around the corridors of hotels we were staying in, surrounded by the degenerates who were supposed to be looking after her, and I worried for her future.'

It didn't help that Whitney was becoming increasingly isolated from family and friends. Her mother Cissy had never approved of the relationship with Bobby, her father John who had continued to provide his daughter with advice and guidance was increasingly side-lined and ultimately Robyn Crawford was pushed out of the inner circle as well.

Reports began to surface that Whitney was displaying a bad attitude to fans and audiences, and journalists discussed her sudden weight loss.

Whitney and Bobby Brown attend the rebirth of the Ocean
Club Resort on December 9, 2000, Paradise Island, Bahamas.

Bobby Brown at Harlem's Apollo Theater, New York New York February 9, 1990

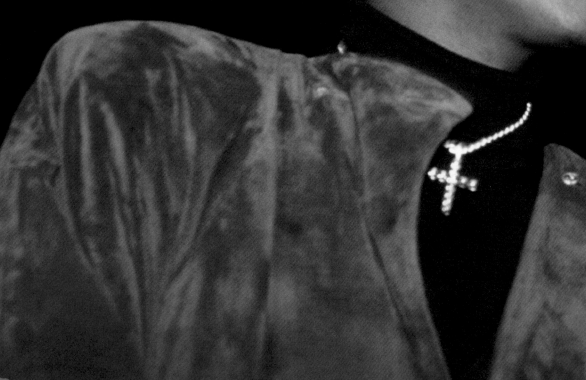

Various police mug shots of Bobby Brown from the 90s

Bobby Brown

Singer, dancer and rapper Bobby Brown began his career as part of R&B / pop group New Edition in 1981 when he was just 12 years old. The five strong group of friends sang and danced in a style similar to Michael Jackson and scored a massive hit with their 1983 hit single *Candy Girl* from their album of the same name.

Bobby left New Edition in 1985 to go solo and became hugely successful as a pioneer of a new sound, a fusion of hip hop and R&B called 'new jack swing'. His second album, *Don't Be Cruel*, was the best-selling album of 1989 and gave him five top 10 singles on the Billboard Hot 100 including a number one with '*My Prerogative*' and a Grammy Award for best Male R&B vocal performance for *Every Little Step*.

It topped the pop and the R&B charts, going on to sell 12 million copies worldwide, making it the bestselling album of 1989. The awards flooded in – a Grammy for Best Male R&B Vocal Performance in February 1990, plus two American Music Awards, a Soul Train Award and a People's Choice Award.

His follow up album *Bobby* was released in 1992. Although it was not as successful as *Don't Be Cruel* commercially it did include the tracks *Humpin' Around*, *Get Away* and *Good Enough* which were reasonably successful singles.

Like his wife, Bobby also tried his hand in the movie business, taking parts in a few films including *A Thin Line Between Love* and *Hate and Two Can Play That Game*. In 1996 he went back to New Edition – which had kept going with new members – for a new album and a tour. He also took part in a reunion album and tour – and repeated the experience for third tour in 2005.

Famously he starred in the reality show *Being Bobby Brown* in 2005 which of course featured Whitney. His 15-year-long marriage to Whitney ended in 2007 when she filed for divorce.

Bobby is a father to seven children, including two who sadly pre-deceased him through drug overdoses - his only daughter with Whitney, Bobbi Kristina died in 2015, and Bobby Brown Jnr, his son from a previous relationship with Kim Ward, died on 18 November 2020.

Bobby told Rolling Stone in 2018 that he had been clean from narcotics for 15 years.

More Movies, Music & Mayhem (1993-2000)

Although matters in her private life were far from smooth, professionally Whitney's career soared throughout the 1990s. As well as being one of the most famous singers on the planet she was now a movie star.

Just months after the birth of her daughter Whitney embarked on a massive world tour, her fourth, this time to promote The Bodyguard soundtrack. Lasting from July 1993 until November 1994, the tour took in the US, South America, Europe, Asia and South Africa.

Once Whitney had finished touring the world and completed a round of award shows where she was showered with accolades, it was time for another starring movie role.

Her follow up to *The Bodyguard* was the 1995 film *Waiting to Exhale* in which she starred as Savannah Jackson, a successful television producer with an unsuccessful love life. Savannah was one of a group of four very different African/American girlfriends who shared their ups and downs and relationships with men, helping each other through their romantic struggles.

At the time it was quite ground-breaking as a film which acknowledged the concerns of affluent black middle-class women. It found an eager audience and grossed more than US$70 million.

Ironically, Whitney was evidently having romantic struggles of her own at the same time. In September, a few months before the film's release at the end of 1995, it was announced that she and Bobby had split up. However, the couple reunited within a few months, although rumours about their rocky relationship would rumble on in the gossip columns for years to come.

Much as Whitney hated the harsh headlines, she did little to calm the situation. Aside from Bobby's various indiscretions and misdemeanours, Whitney herself was gaining a reputation as a rather cold and tough operator.

The *Waiting to Exhale* soundtrack album was produced by 'Babyface' Kenneth Edmonds. It featured a great cast of musical artists led by Whitney who featured on three of the album's 16 tracks. The lead track, *Exhale (Shoop Shoop)*, was number one on the R&B charts and topped the pop charts for a week. The album received 11 Grammy nominations in 1997, including Album of The Year and Song of the Year for *Exhale (Shoop Shoop)*. This hit single made Whitney only the third person ever to have a single debut at number one on the American Billboard chart. It also meant she tied with Madonna in having 11 US number ones in total.

Whitney performs on stage at Mecc, Maastricht, Netherlands, 23rd October 1993

Whitney also featured on *Why Does It Hurt So Bad* and then duetted with CeCe Winans on *Count on Me*. Other featured artists were Aretha Franklin, Toni Braxton, Mary J Blige, Chaka Khan, Faith Evans, Patti LaBelle and Brandy.

Three songs were nominated for Best Female R&B Vocal Performance and *Exhale (Shoop Shoop)* won the Grammy for Best R&B song. The soundtrack sold over 12 million copies worldwide.

Whitney's third film was the 1996 Christmas hit, *The Preacher's Wife* which also spawned a hugely successful album – the original soundtrack from this movie remains the best-selling gospel album of all time.

Directed by Penny Marshall and co-starring Denzel Washington, *The Preacher's Wife* was released in December 1996. It was a remake of a 1947 film called The Bishop's Wife and told the story of a Baptist preacher whose commitment to his duties are affecting his homelife. Whitney played his wife, Julia, who becomes friendly with an angel called Dudley, disguised as a stranger/helper. Played by Denzel Washington, Dudley shows the preacher and his wife how to strike more of a work/life balance.

The film's subplot shows Julia as a star of her husband's church choir. There are then several scenes showcasing gospel music and showing the choir performing. Giving a comic performance in the film as a domineering choir member is Whitney's real life mother Cissy.

With its Christmas storyline, combining elements of religion, classic seasonal songs and gospel music, the film became a huge hit, making $48 million at the box office.

The Los Angeles Times described the film as an 'inspired reworking' of the original, 'warm, sentimental, amusing yet serious'. Whitney won the Best Actress award at the 1997 NAACP Image Awards for her role as Julia – her first and only real acting award. The film was nominated for an Oscar for Best Music, Original Music and Comedy Score.

But even more successful than the film was the original soundtrack album. It debuted at number one on the Billboard Gospel charts, remaining in the top spot for 26 consecutive weeks. In total it stayed in the charts for 117 weeks. The album sold 6m copies worldwide and remains the best-selling gospel album of all time. It was packed with outstanding performances, from Whitney of course, along with guest spots from her mother Cissy, as well as gospel star Shirley Caesar and the Georgia Mass Choir. The tracks were a fabulous mix of traditional and contemporary gospel songs and others with a Christmas flavour. Among the stand-out tracks is Step by Step written by rock star Annie Lennox.

Whitney in a publicity still for the film 'Waiting to Exhale'. 1995

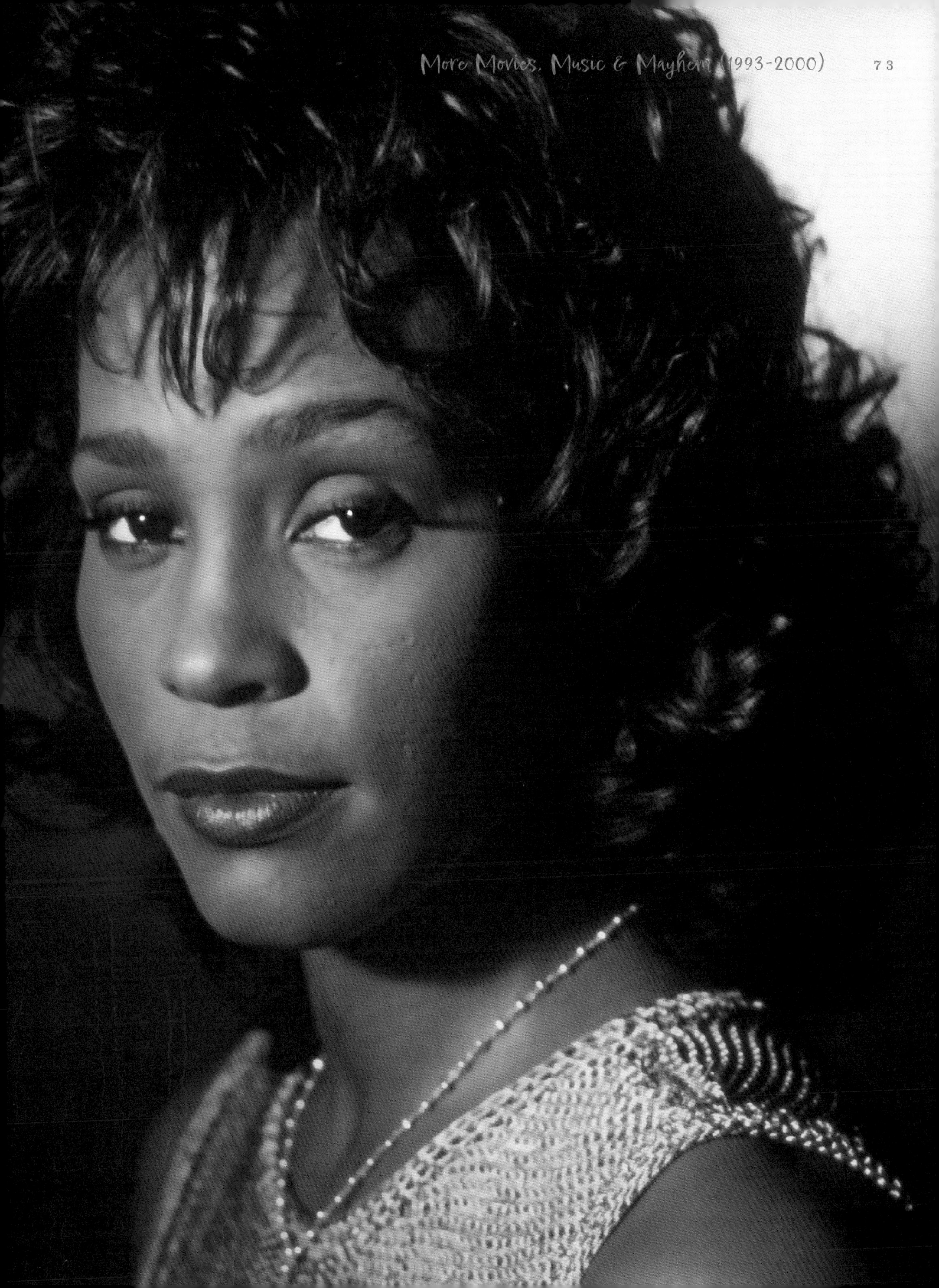

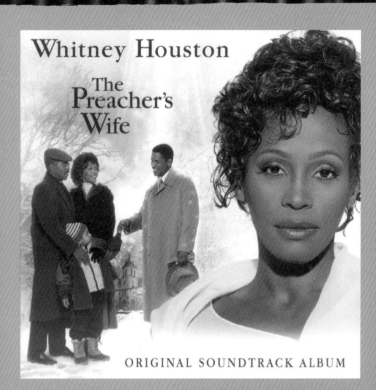

ORIGINAL SOUNDTRACK ALBUM

The Preacher's Wife

Soundtrack album
Released in November 1996 by Arista Records

·

Track list

• I Believe in You and Me (film version)
• Step By Step
• Joy
• Hold on Help is on the Way
• I Go to the Rock
• I Love the Lord
• Somebody Bigger than You and I
• You Were Loved

• My Heart is Calling
• I Believe in You and Me (single version)
• Step by Step (Teddy Riley remix)
• Who Would Imagine a King
• He's All Over Me
• The Lord is my Shepherd
• Joy to the World

Whitney stars in the film 'The Preacher's Wife', 1996

While work was productive and lucrative for Whitney, who was lined up to star in a forthcoming musical version of Cinderella for television, her own real life 'prince', Bobby was having a more torrid time. He had taken a break, ostensibly to focus on his family, but hit the headlines several times including when he was arrested in 1996 for driving under the influence of alcohol, crashed a car and was seen around with other women.

However, in 1997 he got things together and released his fourth studio solo album, *Forever*. It was the only album he produced while he was married to Whitney and it did not do well. The mix of ballads and dance numbers weren't strong enough to compete in what was now a more crowded field dominated by newer artists such as Usher. 'Mr Whitney Houston' was now more famous for his off-stage antics than his musical performances.

Meanwhile Whitney was busy filming the tv movie of *Cinderella* for Walt Disney TV. It was a big production – all singing, all dancing – with beautiful and lavish sets and costumes. Its $US12 million budget made it one of the most expensive television productions ever. The multi-racial cast included singer Brandy as Cinderella, and also starred Whoopi Goldberg as Queen Constantina, and Bernadette Peters as the Wicked Stepmother. Whitney had star billing as the Fairy Godmother, yet to some her performance was disappointing and there were reports that she had been late on set and sometimes uncertain about what she was doing. She played her part as a rather disdainful and superior character, rather than a delightful guardian angel, which didn't come across as amusing, if that's what it was supposed to be.

It aired in November 1997 and attracted an audience of 34 million people who generally loved it. Some reviews were less enthusiastic, including *Entertainment Weekly* which included the line that; 'Whitney Houston, however – once upon a time slated to play the Cinderella role herself in this production – strikes a wrong note as a sassy, vaguely hostile fairy godmother'. And the review in *Variety* found Whitney's portrayal of the Fairy Godmother to be a 'frightening caricature, one certain to send the kids scurrying into Mom's lap for reassurance that the good woman will soon go away'.

In a chat show interview the following year, Whitney seemed very keen to distance herself from suggestions that she was a role model for young girls around the world.

'I am not a role model,' she said emphatically. 'No, that role model thing is scary, scary. I would just really like to be an example of what can be done if you put your mind and your work and your body and your soul into it – and that's it. This is my life and not to be looked at as a role. This is my life. And I'm certainly not a role model.'

Cinderella promotional still of Brandy Norwood & Whitney, 1997

Turning back to her music career proper, Whitney's next album was the 1998 release, *My Love Is Your Love*, her fourth studio album, and her first in eight years. She threw everything at it with 13 tracks taking in R&B, reggae, pop and soul – even some hip hop.

It was another huge global hit, selling 10 million copies worldwide and is widely regarded as among her best work. Although slightly less popular in the US, it still went four times platinum. Some commentators found the album a little confusing stylistically, believing that fans of her ballads were not necessarily admirers of the hip hop numbers she had introduced.

Among the hit singles it produced came the duet with Mariah Carey, *When You Believe*, from *The Prince of Egypt* movie soundtrack, which won an Academy award for its writers: *Heartbreak Hotel* featuring Kelly Price and Faith Evans and the up-tempo *It's Not Right But It's Okay*. Then of course, the title track, *My Love Is Your Love*, became a huge hit for her.

The album was supported with another round of tv shows and a successful world tour of over 60 shows in North America and Europe during 1999

Whitney performs during an AmFar Benefit Concert.
New York New York December 1998

Whitney Houston
my love is
your love

My Love is Your Love

Whitney's fourth studio album
Released in November 1998 by Arista Records

Track list

- It's Not Right But It's Okay
- Heartbreak Hotel
(ft Faith Evans and Kelly Price)
- My Love is Your Love
- When You Believe
(from The Prince of Egypt Soundtrack)
- If I Told You That
- In My Business

(ft Missy Misdemeanour Elliott)
- I Learned From The Best
- Oh Yes
- Get It Back
- Until You Come Back
- I Bow Out
- You'll Never Stand Alone
- I Was Made To Love Him

But it was during this tour that cracks began to show in Whitney's carefully cultivated public image. It had been an open secret within the industry that Whitney was troubled and had been increasing her use of drugs for a while. She had also begun to display somewhat erratic and unreliable behaviour.

But now her voice was also showing the strain and audiences could hear for themselves the toll her unhealthy lifestyle was taking

As the tour went on Bobby Brown became a bigger part of the act. The first musical collaboration between the couple had been back in 1992 when their duet, the up-tempo *We've Got Something In Common* was featured on Bobby's album, called *Bobby* . It was also featured on his 1993 compilation album *Remixes In The Key of B*. During their marriage he would join her on stage from time to time – not always in peak performance mode. He was apt to join her on stage more frequently during the 1999 tour.

Off-stage there were continual fallouts between Bobby and Robyn Crawford. The two of them were complete opposites and to an extent were vying for Whitney's attention – Robyn as her long-time best friend and confidante, Bobby as her husband. Both heartily disliked the other and would prefer it when they were not around. Things between them came to a head in Germany when Robyn suddenly left the tour and Whitney's entourage, with no public explanation. Whitney had also lost the services of her long-term, real-life bodyguard David Roberts a few years earlier. Roberts claims that his services were dispensed with after he wrote a letter to Whitney's lawyers outlining his concerns about her drugs use following a disastrous tour of Singapore.

It seemed that Whitney was missing Robyn and David Roberts – two major pillars of support

Evidently struggling to complete the tour, Whitney was becoming increasingly unreliable and in fact cancelled five shows during her 1999 tour, citing throat problems as the cause. One of these was a last-minute cancellation of a massive sold-out show in her hometown of Newark, New Jersey. Whitney was one of the few artists in the world at the time who could command upwards of $US100 per ticket – often charging as much as $150 – so a cancellation was a big deal and some venues demanded compensation.

Whitney at The 19th BRIT Awards, London Arena, London, UK, Tuesday 16 February 1999

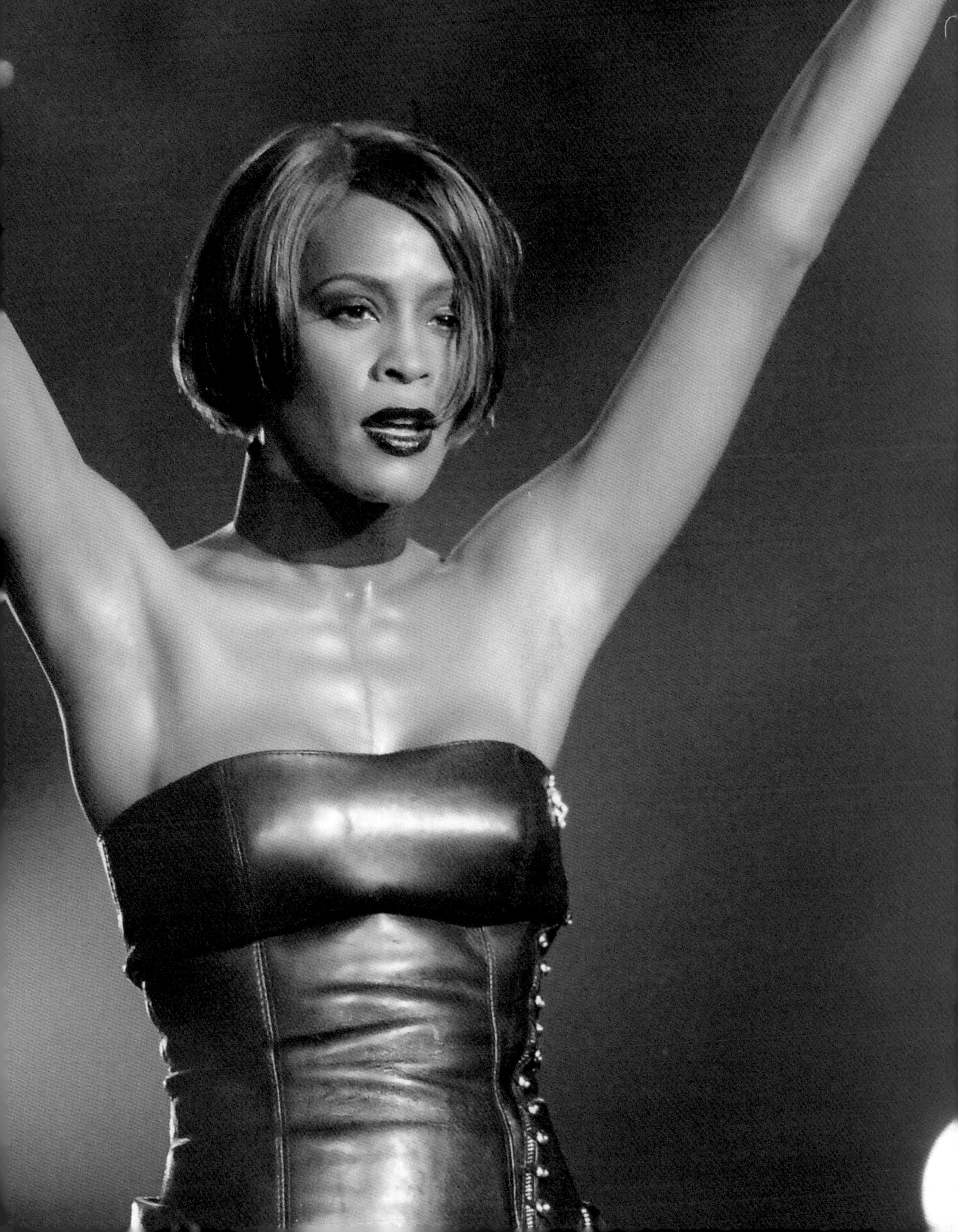

Whitney during 1999 MTV Europe Music Awards

Whitney performing in 2000

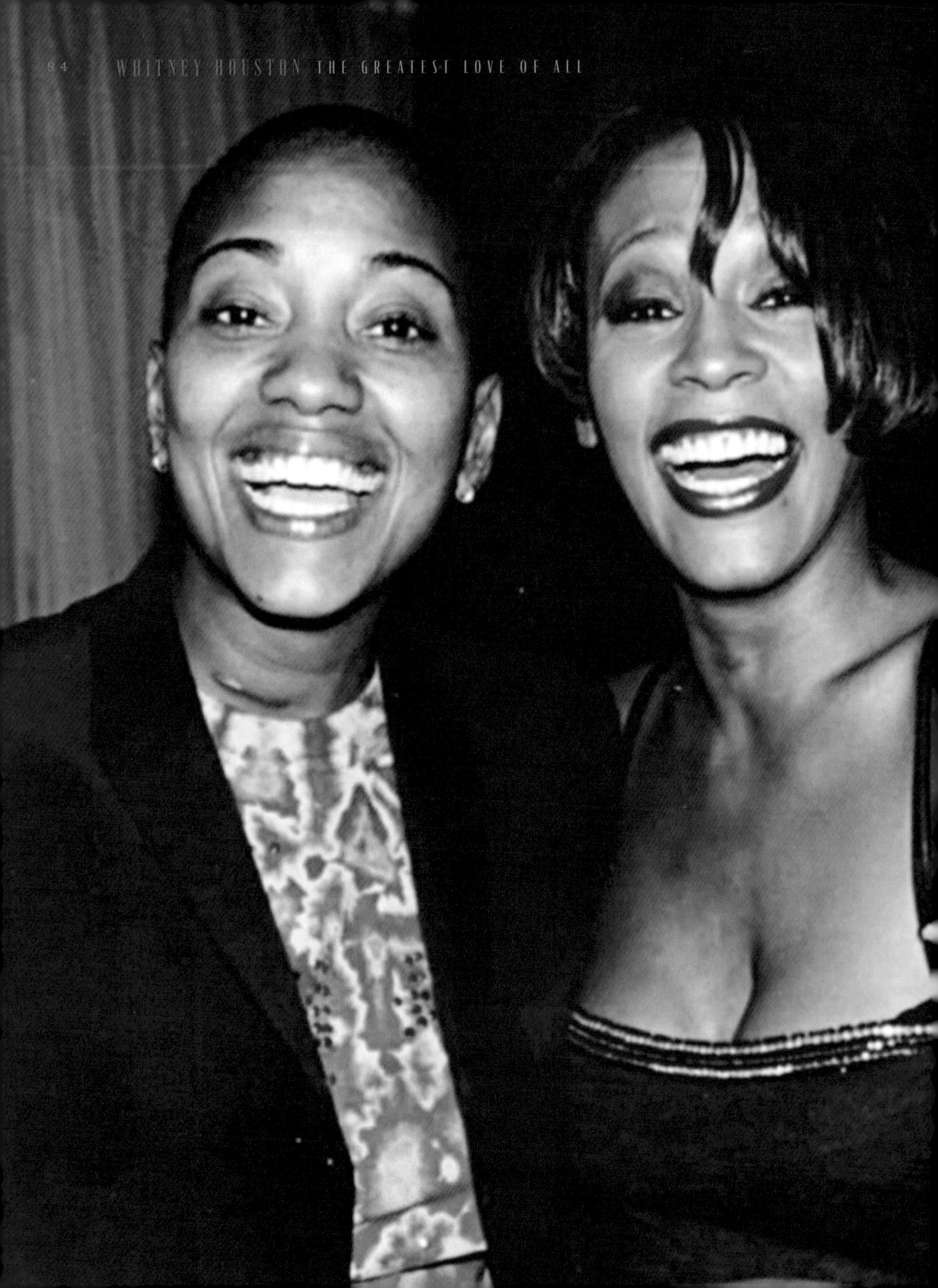

Whitney's eventual downfall seems to date from around this time. It seemed that Robyn was keeping the show on the road, and helping Whitney stay on the straight and narrow. Without Robyn, Whitney turned increasingly to drugs as the crutch to get her through and her drug use spiralled.

With this came a lot of guilt. Whitney had always believed that her voice was a gift from God and became very ashamed that she was not taking care of it. She seemingly couldn't help herself though. She truly loved Bobby and believed that he understood and accepted her.

Those 1999 concerts made up what would be her last successful world tour. Although her voice was still ridiculously good compared to most people - unparalleled in fact - her relentless schedule and unhealthy off-stage habits were naturally having a negative effect.

Her saxophonist on the tour, Kirk Whalum, said; There was a timbre, a sound, to her voice which was just angelic. But she wasn't taking care of herself... [on tour] we had to lower the key of the songs.

Whitney & Robyn Crawford in a scene from the promo for the ©Miramax documentary, Whitney, 2018

From bad to worse (2000-2011)

The new millennium was not a new dawn for Whitney. Looking thin and unhealthy, frequently wearing wigs to disguise hair loss, she had gained a bad reputation. She was increasingly late for engagements, then she couldn't necessarily deliver on the occasions when she did arrive. She was even a 'no show' at the Rock and Roll Hall of Fame event that March when she was scheduled to perform and present the award to honour her mentor Clive Davis.

In January 2000 Whitney was travelling from Hawaii to San Francisco when she was discovered to be carrying 15.2 grams of marijuana. Security guards at the airport confiscated her bag but had no power to arrest her. While they were waiting for police to arrive Whitney managed to board her plane, claiming afterwards that she didn't understand 'the fuss' about a small amount of pot. The misdemeanour meant that she was 'wanted' in Hawaii but the island would not go through the trouble and expense of an extradition. However, journalists made hay with the story.

One particularly low spot was a planned appearance at the 72nd Academy awards ceremony in 2000. Reports from those at the rehearsals on the Friday before the Sunday show said it was apparent that her voice was suffering, her timing was off and that she couldn't get to grips with the staging and performance. The event was to be broadcast live around the world to millions of viewers and producers decided that they couldn't take a risk on Whitney and so replaced her.

The Los Angeles Times published the following report at the time:

'Prominent among the questions: Where was singer Whitney Houston, who had been scheduled to perform in a medley of old Oscar-nominated songs along with Garth Brooks, Ray Charles and Queen Latifah?

'Several sources said Houston was "fired" by orchestra leader Burt Bacharach during a rehearsal Friday, where she reportedly was unprepared and unresponsive to direction. Country singer Faith Hill filled in for Houston during the Oscars.

'Neither Bacharach nor Houston could be reached for comment. But show publicist Jane LaBonte said Houston was having obvious problems with her voice during the Friday rehearsal, and was unsure on Saturday whether she would be well enough to perform Sunday. "She was having a very hard time singing," said LaBonte. "It was very clear that her voice was in trouble".'

Whitney at the 2000 Grammy Awards held in LA

That same spokeswoman assured *Hollywood.com* website that Whitney had not been fired, saying, 'She didn't feel good. She was having problems with her voice. Whitney decided that at the end, she wasn't going to risk it and be in the show. She bowed out.'

Whatever the true story, it was becoming more and more apparent to those in the industry, as well as to Whitney's fans, that her career was beginning to unravel. However, at the beginning of the 2000s, Whitney was still living off the success of her *Your Love is My Love album*. During the awards season she was voted Female Artist of the Decade at the Soul Train Awards – a pleasing turnaround from the booing of the late 1980s – and also picked up the Grammy award for Best R&B Female Vocal performance for *It's Not Right But It's Okay*.

Whitney had other public difficulties at a party to celebrate the 25th anniversary of Arista records that year. Her set was a medley of her biggest hits, which went quite well other than she was having problems with her full-length gold sequinned dress, almost tripping over it and then clutching it up towards her as she sang. Then the performance came to an odd end as she was joined on stage by Bobby for *My Love is Your Love* and the pair seemed in a world of their own as they jammed and jumped around – it was all rather disorderly. Gossip magazines were full of chatter about Whitney's friends and colleagues at the party being concerned for her welfare. The papers were also running stories about rows between Whitney and her parents regarding the welfare of little Bobbi Kristina. Cissy and John were reportedly considering an 'intervention' if Whitney and Bobby didn't clean up their act and their relationship with their daughter became fraught as a result.

Arista Records was going through some turbulence of its own. Shortly after the company released the double disc album *Whitney Houston: The Greatest Hits* the company was sold to the German entertainment company Bertelsmann Music Group. Whitney's mentor Clive Davis lost his position as Arista's president and was replaced by L.A. Reid.

This meant there was of course a question mark over Whitney's future recording career. Would she stay with Arista or follow Clive who was setting up a new label called J Records. Would he want her with him at his new label?

Whitney was still in a reasonably strong position professionally. Despite her personal difficulties, her Greatest Hits album had topped the charts in the UK and made top five in America. Worldwide it sold over eight million copies – her fans were obviously still inclined to celebrate her talent and her music from the past 15-plus years of stardom.

Whitney performs at Arista Records 25th anniversary gala concert at the Shrine Auditorium, April 2000

Whitney Houston: The Greatest Hits

Released in May 2000 by Arista Records

Track list

Disc one

- Saving All My Love For You
- Greatest Love of All
- All at Once
- If You Say My Eyes are Beautiful (with Jermaine Jackson)
- Didn't We Almost Have It All
- Where Do Broken Hearts Go
- All The Man That I Need
- Run to You
- I Have Nothing
- I Will Always Love You
- Exhale (Shoop Shoop)
- Why Does It Hurt So Bad
- I Believe in You And Me
- Heartbreak Hotel (ft Faith Evans and Kelly Price)
- My Love is Your Love
- Same Script, Different Cast
- Could I Have This Kiss Forever (with Enrique Iglesias)

Disc two

- Fine
- If I Told You That
- It's Not Right But It's Okay – Thunderpuss Mix
- My Love is Your Love
- Heartbreak Hotel (ft Faith Evans and Kelly Price)
- I Learned from the Best – HQ2 Radio Mix
- Step By Step Junior Vasquez Tribal X Beats
- I'm Every Woman – C+C Club Mix Radio Edit
- Queen of the Night – CJ's Single Edit
- I Will Always Love You – Hex Hector Radio Mix
- Love Will Save The Day – Jellybean & David Morales Mix
- I'm Your Baby Tonight – Dronez Club Mix
- So Emotional – David Morales Mix
- I Wanna Dance with Somebody (Who Loves me) Junior Vasquez Mix
- How Will I Know – Junior Vasquez Club Mix
- Greatest Love of All – Junior Vasquez Mix
- One Moment in Time
- The Star Spangled Banner (ft. The Florida Orchestra)

Whitney performs during the 1st Annual BET Awards, Paris
Hotel and Casino in Las Vegas, June 19, 2001

Lots of things were up in the air for Whitney at that time. As well as the changes at Arista, Bobby was continuing to make all the wrong types of headlines. In the early summer he spent time in jail in Ft Lauderdale, Florida, after being refused bail while awaiting trial for a historical charge of violating bail terms back in 1999 which had just caught up with him.

With Bobby temporarily out of the picture, Whitney's friends and family reportedly tried to persuade her to leave him and clean up her act. But nothing worked in the long term and once Bobby was free again, he and Whitney picked up their old life and bad habits, including cocaine, according to reports in magazines such as *National Enquirer*. The couple stayed at the Grandover Resort in North Carolina that summer and the *Enquirer* reported a member of staff as saying; 'You'd think they'd know better. The smell of marijuana from their suite was drifting into the hallway. It was sickening, their daughter was staying right across the hall in another suite... There was also evidence that cocaine was used in the suite. On the bathroom counter lay an empty package of baking soda and a spoon with burn marks on the bottom, necessary items to free-base cocaine'. There were to be reports of other such binges in the years to come.

As well as missing Robyn Crawford and bodyguard David Roberts, Whitney also suffered another professional loss when her personal physician Dr Julian Groff died. He took care of her voice, sometimes travelling with her. Now he too was gone and Whitney's voice was losing power and becoming less reliable.

Her ongoing substance abuse problem was becoming increasingly difficult to hide, not least because her appearance was suffering; she looked thin and unhealthy.

There was a huge hullabaloo after Whitney appeared on national television during a tribute concert for Michael Jackson in New York in 2001. She looked incredibly gaunt, even emaciated, and fans and commentators were shocked. Her voice was also under par and raspy. One newspaper described her as looking like 'a walking skeleton'.

Later Whitney was to make further admissions about her drugs use, famously in a 2009 interview with Oprah Winfrey. But, for now, she had other things to worry about – not least of which was a legal case brought against her by her father's company.

Her father John had remained key in Whitney's life and remained her trusted advisor, even after his divorce from Cissy in 1990. Whitney frequently turned to him for help when she had problems or a new contract to negotiate.

Whitney at the Songwriters Hall of Fame 32nd Annual Awards, The Sheraton New York Hotel and Towers, June 14, 2001

Although she admitted they had some disagreements, she always said she remained close to him, for example in an interview when she said; 'We've hollered and screamed at each other. But it was always over business. If it were anything else, I would not be screaming at my father . . . I'll never find anyone to love me like my daddy does. I will always be daddy's girl.'

But the strain in their relationship came to a head in August 2002 when John Houston Enterprises filed a breach-of-contract suit in the New Jersey Superior Court. According to MTV, the suit said that Whitney had failed to pay her father's company for management services including sorting out some legalities surrounding her 2000 marijuana episode in Hawaii airport when she was stopped for possession (the charges were ultimately dropped) and negotiating her contract renewal with Arista.

While the elder Houston is not named in the suit, company president Kevin Skinner told MTV he was a co-plaintiff, saying; 'We weren't her managers per se, at least not in name. But we were in effect. She had no management at that time, and we masterminded the whole situation. All of the parties involved, we selected. And we did whatever it took to get her [financially solvent]. It took her five years to run through her money, and it took us five weeks to get it back. But we didn't do it for free.'

Another theory surrounding the lawsuit was that John wanted the $100 million so that he could protect it by putting it aside for his daughter to use at a later date, rather than have her spend it all on drugs and wild living. Adding credibility to this is the fact that the lawsuit included an injunction requiring Whitney to put 20 per cent of her earnings into a trust – a rainy day fund almost - should her career end.

Not that Whitney was currently short of work – but she was getting through cash at a rate of knots. In August 2001 she had signed a further deal with Arista under its new boss L.A. Reid. One of Reid's most expensive decisions came when he gave her a new contract worth a reported $100m in 2001. Whitney received an advance of $25 million with the further $75 million contingent on the production of six new albums and two compilations.

Her first album under this deal was *Just Whitney* released in 2002. In the United States it debuted at #9 on the Billboard 200 and #3 in the R&B chart, while only making it to #76 in the UK. The mix of soul-orientated, ballads, mid-tempo and dance numbers got a mixed reception from reviewers.

The best reviews, such as this from the BBC in the UK, commended Whitney for a 'return to her former glory with a combination of high-voltage ballads and smooth-liqueur R&B' and praised her for having 'one of the most exceptional voices in contemporary music'.

Whitney & Mary J. Blige perform at the VH1 Divas Las Vegas May 22 2002

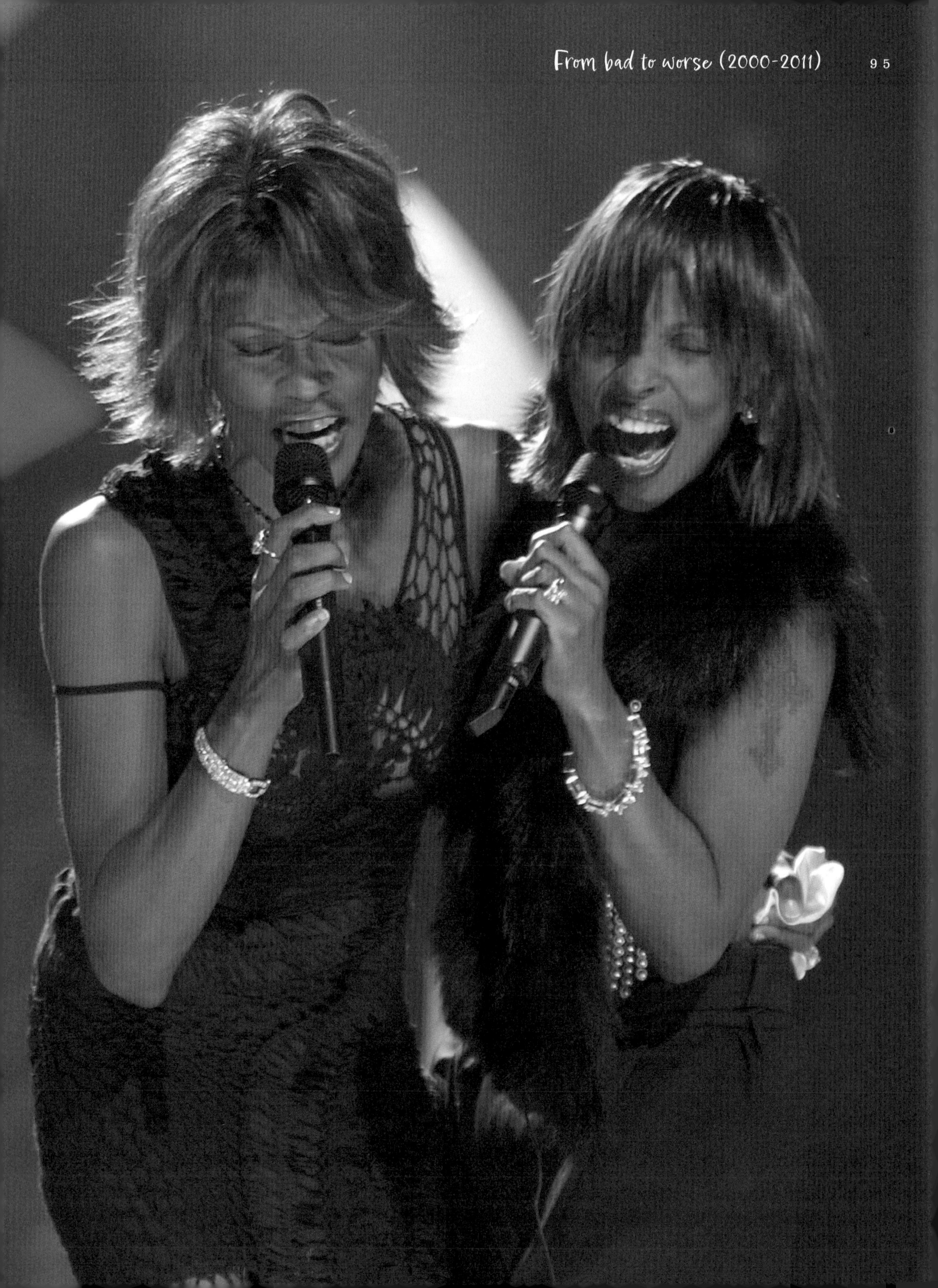

However, the less favourable reviews, such as in *USA Today* said; 'At her best, Houston is full of sass and attitude and, most of all, joy. But with so much emphasis on what's bothering her, you can't help but wonder whether the thrill is gone.' And according to *The Guardian* in the UK, 'the album takes 'a musical step backwards'.

Most could agree however that it was a more personal album than she had ever before produced. For example, the first single from the album *'Whatchulookinat'* took a pop at the press coverage of her marriage to Bobby and included the lyrics, 'They're watching your every move...Trying to mess with my concentration, don't even have a clue of what I'm facing, all you know you need to stop it, defaming my name for a profit', and 'Same spotlight that gave me fame, trying to dirty up Whitney's name'.

She was also plainly aiming to quash rumours about her marriage problems by duetting with Bobby on My Love.

Just Whitney

**Whitney's fifth studio album
Released in December 2002 by Arista Records**

Track list

- **One Of Those Days**
- **Tell Me No**
- **Things You Say**
- **My Love (ft Bobby Brown)**
- **Love That Man**
- **Try It On My Own**
- **Dear John Letter**
- **Unashamed**
- **You Light Up My Life**
- **Whatchulookinat – Main (AKA Backing Vox Up)**

Whitney & Bobby Brown perform at the VH1 Divas
Las Vegas May 22 2002

In an ill-advised appearance to promote the album, and presumably lacking in decent PR advice, Whitney gave an interview to ABC's Diane Sawyer during which she admitted that she had experimented with drugs and alcohol. Asked whether she had abused alcohol, marijuana, cocaine or pills, she said: 'It has been at times'. Apparently double-checking she had understood correctly, Diane Sawyer said, 'All?' And Whitney replied, 'At times'.

'If you had to name the devil for you, the biggest devil among them?' pressed Ms Sawyer. And Whitney replied, 'That would be me. It's my deciding, it's my heart, it's what I want. And what I don't want. Nobody makes me do anything I don't want to do. It's my decision. So the biggest devil is me. I'm either my best friend or my worst enemy. And that's how I have to deal with it.' However, Whitney vehemently denied ever taking crack cocaine, saying; 'Let's get one thing straight, crack is cheap. I make too much to ever smoke crack. Let's get that straight. OK? We don't do crack. We don't do that. Crack is wack.'

Her 'crack is wack' line was to haunt her for years to come, with comedians using it to make jokes about her. Basically, she was denying drug use by saying that she could afford 'better' drugs.

Sadly, narcotics still loomed large in Whitney and Bobby's private life. Incidents of serious misuse were reported in the press including some frightening sounding occasions when, at different times, both of them had needed hospital treatment to save their lives.

Then Whitney suffered a terrible emotional blow when her father died, before their lawsuit was settled. John suffered a cardiac arrest after a lengthy battle with diabetes and heart disease, and died on 2 February 2003 in Manhattan. Announcing the news, Whitney's publicist said that the legal problems between the two had not affected the father and daughter's personal relationship. However, Whitney had spoken of it during her interview with Diane Sawyer and described it as 'hurtful'.

However, Whitney arrived in New York from Miami, where she had been shooting a magazine cover and according to the spokeswoman; 'The entire Houston family and John loved each other very, very much and each and every one of them had a chance to be with John (at the end).'

Whitney performs at the 'VH1 Divas Las Vegas' May 22 2002

After John's death, and in an attempt to deal with it, along with her substance abuse, her volatile marriage and consequently strained relationships with family and friends, Whitney tried to sort out her life by attending a drug rehabilitation facility. A statement from her publicist said simply that Whitney thanked everyone for 'their support and prayers'.

It evidently wasn't a complete success as further stints in rehab were to follow. But in the short-term Whitney felt strong enough to take part in a reality show with her husband called *Being Bobby Brown*. It was aired during July and August 2005 and centred on the couple's homelife as they managed work and home and bringing up Bobbi Kristina and Bobby's other children.

If any of her fans had been in any doubt as to Whitney's true state of mind and behaviour patterns at this time, the tv show made it all crystal clear. The programme did not show the couple in a flattering light – at times it was shocking, showing too much graphic detail and some outrageous behaviour. The original 10 episodes were all shot between January to June 2005 and then an 11th was compiled using previously unseen footage, much of it focussing more on Whitney than Bobby.

After one scene where Whitney is shown to be irritated and bad-tempered with fans asking for pictures and autographs, Bobby explains to viewers that he believed her behaviour stemmed from a deep desire for privacy – greater than his own. Commenting on the incident where Whitney is almost rude to onlookers, saying; 'I'm eating, can you see that I'm eating?' Bobby explains to camera that while he got into the business because of 'people, she [Whitney] got into it to sing. 'You want a picture with me, that's cool,' he said. 'You want a pic with Whitney – I doubt it'.

There was never a second series and Whitney withheld permission for a DVD release.

A year later, following more rows and rumours of Bobby's liaisons with other women, Whitney decided she needed out of her marriage and began proceedings for a legal separation, along with full custody of their daughter Bobbi Kristina. The couple were finally divorced in 2007, with Whitney gaining custody of Bobbi Kristina as she had wanted.

Speaking afterwards during her 2009 interview with Oprah Winfrey she explained how she finally realised that their marriage was doomed. "I just knew, I was like, 'You don't smell right, you don't look right, something is going on.' And then all this other stuff started coming out.' Referencing stories about Bobbi's history with other women she said eventually she had to discover the truth. 'I checked, I checked. I didn't look for it. But I checked.' Houston said she then began removing herself from their home little by little.

Around the time of her divorce Whitney was seen back in company of Clive Davis and rumours of a comeback swirled around. Whitney began to look better than she had in years. But it was not all plain sailing. There continued to be times when her voice let her down during live performances.

The word was that her soaring, sweeping vocal flourishes and soft, sweet tones were disappearing, along with her warm stage presence and captivating performances.

The three-octave range was no more, she didn't have the stamina to hold notes as she used to - even her speaking voice was sounding harsh and raspy

Whitney was of course aware of all this, which only served to add to the pressures on her. As well as wanting to do well for her fans, she was also acutely aware that huge numbers of people in her entourage and recording and stage production crews relied on her for their living. On top of all that her religious upbringing made her feel that she had let God down by failing to take care of her 'instrument'. This could only add to her inclination to self-medicate to try and make herself feel better. It was a vicious circle.

However, despite her struggles, Whitney still had many professional obligations, not least of which was the fulfilment of her multi-album deal with Arista. She and the company were working on new material, which was originally set for release at the end of 2007, although various delays pushed it back to September 2009.

Entitled, *I Look to You*, the album was eagerly anticipated by fans as a triumphant comeback, a return to form by their beloved diva. Over her divorce and the associated problems, they were confident that Whitney could pick up and again reach the dazzling heights she had achieved in the 1980s and 1990s.

Key to their faith that Whitney revive her career successfully was the news that her album was being overseen by her long-time friend and mentor Clive Davis. Clive was now back at Arista because his J Records label had been acquired by Sony, who following their merger with BMG, now owned the Arista label.

As he had done during their early years together, Clive took time and care over the album and organised a gentle promotion schedule to ease Whitney back into the spotlight, including small but classy 'listening parties' for critics. This was all part of a charm offensive to display Whitney's new cleaned-up image and entirely necessary following the terrible headlines and the disaster of the *Being Bobby Brown* television series.

Clive also oversaw the selection of songs for the album and put together a top team of producers which included younger talents including Alicia Keys and will.i.am. Also on the team was David Foster, who had worked on Whitney's big hit, *I Will Always Love You* from *The Bodyguard*. His inclusion on the production team was evidently a lucky omen which seemed to pay off when *I Look To You* gave Whitney her first number one album since *The Bodyguard* soundtrack 15 years earlier.

Whitney's seventh and final studio album
Released in 2009 by Arista Records

Track list

- Million Dollar Bill
- Nothin' But Love
- Call You Tonight
- I Look To You
- Like I Never Left (ft Akon)
- A Song For You
- I Didn't Know My Own Strength
- Worth It
- For The Lovers
- I Got You
- Salute

Whitney performs at the 2009 GRAMMY Salute To
Industry Icons honoring Clive Davis at the Beverly Hilton
Hotel on February 7, 2009

I Look to You sold 304,000 copies during its first week on sale, catapulting Whitney back to the top of the charts with the best debut week of her career.

Music critics generally welcomed Whitney's return and were keen to be kind about the music, although many referenced the change in her singing voice.

'It is a modern soul record', said *Rolling Stone* magazine's review. 'A collection of sleek, often spunky, love songs that aim at something more immediate and tangible than nostalgia or catharsis: Houston wants back in the diva stakes'.

Many reviews particularly praised the opening track, and first American single, Million Dollar Bill, which was co-written by Alicia Keys.

Writing for the BBC review, Lloyd Bradley said he also liked the first couple of tracks in particular, before going on to lament the fact that then the album majored on the 'identikit power ballads' with which Whitney had made her name. He wrote; 'It all starts off well enough, with the opening track, *Million Dollar Bill*, setting the singer against a very modern-sounding background, but one with enough depth and actual musical substance to balance the size of her voice. It's like old-school soul only with up-to-date instruments. It's so precisely where Whitney should be that she sounds totally energised, sparring with the backing vocals and having fun inside a superbly funky arrangement. The next track, *Nothin' But Love*, takes a sparser, synthier approach but provides more than enough to give her a decent platform to work from and keeps things up-tempo fun and vocally playful.'

'Although *I Look to You* does drag itself back to the present day with later tracks *Worth It* and *For the Lovers*, on which she sounds like she's enjoying herself again, especially on the elastic grooves of the latter, at this point it only shows up that middle section retreat into her safety zone as being even more unnecessary.'

Several of the lyrics referenced Whitney's well-publicised struggles, giving her a platform to explain some of what she had been through and demonstrate the strength which was carrying her through. As she told reporters, this latest album reflected her emotional state and chronicled events in her personal life since her last musical release in 2002.

Publicity Photo of Whitney for 2009 Album

'That makes it real' she said. 'The changes that we go through, the transitions that we go through, the tests that we go through, being a mother, becoming a single mother. It all had its ups and its downs, but for the most part, I kept my faith and I kept my head up... I took my time. All the triumphs and the ups and downs and stuff, it's all incorporated on the album, and hopefully not only does it inspire me, but inspires a whole lot of other people'.

With a new hit album under her belt, it was standard to follow it up with a concert tour – hence the announcement of the *Nothing But Love* 50-date world tour scheduled for December 2009 to June 2010, taking in Asia, Australia and Europe.

But now came questions about Whitney's preparation and stamina. Things got underway calmly enough, but within a few months, when the tour rolled into Australia, things were evidently amiss in her live performances. It was her first visit to the continent in 22 years, so an eager audience awaited her – but they were disappointed, largely by Whitney's evident vocal difficulties.

For example, *The Daily Telegraph* reported that; 'in Sydney, ...[Whitney's] acoustic set of old favourites unfortunately could not hide the very obvious problems with her voice, the strain and those coughs that punctuated the Brisbane show were back. By the time she got to the gospel section of the show a steady stream of disappointed, saddened and angry fans started streaming out the doors.'

The terrible press reports continued once the tour reached Europe and her shows were mauled by critics. Financially it did the business, grossing some US$36 million, but it left fans disappointed and presumably less likely to buy another ticket in the future.

As it turned out there was no chance to test this theory as *Nothing But Love* was to be her last tour. Whitney was back in rehab within months of returning home. Her spokeswoman confirmed that Whitney was in an outpatient rehab program for drug and alcohol treatment, stating that, 'Whitney voluntarily entered the program to support her long-standing recovery process.'

Whitney had again admitted publicly, after her 2002 Diane Sawyer interview, to using drugs in a two-part interview with Oprah Winfrey in 2009.

She said then that marijuana laced with cocaine was the substance of choice while she was with Bobby and they "would have ounces" of cocaine available at all times. She also discussed her marriage and said that her vows had been sacred to her. 'I never cheated, I never did none of that stuff,' she told Winfrey. 'I just did the drugs.'

Whitney performs on stage at Acer Arena on February 24, 2010 in Sydney, Australia

Although now free of Bobby and the marriage, she was evidently still struggling

Following this latest stint of rehab, Whitney emerged with news that she had a new and exciting project. It was another film role, starring alongside American Idol winner Jordin Sparks in a musical movie *Sparkle*.

Inspired by the true story of the 1960s hit Motown girl group The Supremes, *Sparkle* was a remake of the 1976 movie of the same name. Whitney was an executive producer as well as taking a starring role as a character called Emma Anderson who was the strict mother of the three sisters in the group. It was a great fit for her as her character 'Emma' was a born-again church lady. The aspect that didn't ring true was that before becoming a mother she had failed at a career in the entertainment industry. The soundtrack's first official lead single was the last song recorded by Whitney before she died - a duet with Jordin Sparks called *Celebrate*.

Sparkle was her fifth feature film, and as things turned out, her final movie performance. Filming took place during 2011 and all seemed to go well. The movie's producer, Howard Rosenman, told *Entertainment Weekly* that he couldn't speak highly enough of Whitney in her final big-screen role.

She is unbelievably brilliant in it,' he said, adding that she had appeared 'healthy' and 'spirited' on the set and was totally into a 'pro' mode'.

She is just incandescent and brilliant [in the film] and was on her way to make this huge comeback,' he said. 'She was fabulous on the set, she was beloved by the crew, she was a total professional.'

The end (2012)

s 2012 began, it appeared that Whitney was finally in a good place again. She was working hard to improve her voice, her film Sparkle was in pre-production and rumours were swirling that she was being lined up to become a mentor on US talent series The X Factor.

But before anything was confirmed, tragedy struck - Whitney was found dead in her bath on 11 February, 2012 in the Beverley Hills Hilton hotel, California. It was the eve of that year's Grammy awards and she was getting ready for a pre-awards party hosted by her beloved mentor Clive Davis. Her assistant Mary Jones discovered her and immediately called for help. Her bodyguard and brother-in-law Ray Watson attempted CPR, but it was too late. The cause of death was later found to be accidental drowning with atherosclerotic heart disease and cocaine abuse as contributing factors. Whitney was 48 years old.

Clive Davis's pre-Grammy party still went ahead because, as he told guests, Whitney loved music and loved this night that celebrated music. He said he believed that Whitney would have asked that the music go on and that her family wanted the party to go on. He said later that he was 'personally devastated by the loss of someone who has meant so much to me for so many years'.

The following night's Grammy Awards show included a tribute to Whitney led by Jennifer Hudson and Chaka Khan, including a performance of *I Will Always Love You*.

Meanwhile tributes poured in from a shocked industry. Dolly Parton said, 'Mine is only one of the millions of hearts broken over the death of Whitney Houston. I will always be grateful and in awe of the wonderful performance she did on my song, and I can truly say from the bottom of my heart, 'Whitney, I will always love you. You will be missed".'

Broadcaster and music journalist Paul Gambaccini described Whitney's voice as 'the template for female vocal performers for the last 30 years'.

Aretha Franklin, speaking to Rolling Stone magazine, said, '...Whitney's mother taught her how to be a fighter. On her last tour, she had lost the top range of her voice, and some of the audiences were not very kind. But night after night, she stood there like a champion and gave her very best. She seemed to be getting it back – I saw some of the previews for Sparkle, and she really looked great, fresh and healthy. So when the news came out she had passed, I was stunned. I just couldn't believe it.

'Gospel was Whitney's foundation and background. She was raised on the Word and she certainly praised the Lord. The rest of it just wasn't that important. One of Whitney's favourite songs was "Yes, Jesus Loves Me." And if Jesus loves you, what is more important than that?'

And of course the most touching tribute of them all came from her mother Cissy who wrote the following obituary.

Dearest Whitney,

The presence of God blessed our home with life, love, joy and peace. You and your brothers were the centre of divine love, attracting God's richest blessings. You were a child of God. We had so much love in our home that was truly from on high.

You always gave without expecting anything in return and our love was the force at multiplied these blessings higher and higher. I never told you but when you were born the Holy Spirit told me that you would not be with me long. And I thank God for the beautiful flower he allowed me to raise and cherish for 48 years.

God said it's time Nippy; your work is done. The other day on February 11 He came for you. But not without warning. For two months now I have been depressed, crying, lonesome and sad, not knowing why.

On Saturday, before I found out about your transition, my doorbell rang. I went to answer it but there was no one there. It rang again and again, no one was there. I called the concierge to tell him someone was ringing my doorbell. He checked the cameras and told me that no one was there. You promised me you were coming to spend time with me after the Grammys. I believe the spirits allowed you to come after all.

I love you Nippy and how I miss you, your beautiful smile, your special little things you used to say to me and sometimes you'd call just to say Hi Mommie, I love you so much. I loved you so much more.
I love you.
I'll miss you.
Thank you for being such a wonderful daughter.
Rest my baby girl in Peace, you're now in the arms of Jesus.

Love, Mommie

Speaking later and looking back on Whitney's life, Cissy said; 'I am very proud of my daughter. She accomplished a whole lot in the short time that she had here. She was a very wonderful person.'

Whitney had said that she wanted to be remembered as 'someone who cared'. That was certainly the case at her funeral service at the New Hope Baptist Church in her hometown of Newark, New Jersey, where tributes were paid to her in a service scheduled to last for two hours, but actually running for almost four hours. It was a televised and invitation-only memorial on 18 February 2012.

Among those who performed at the funeral were Stevie Wonder, CeCe Winans, Alicia Keys, Kim Burrell and R. Kelly. There were also hymns from the church choir. Clive Davis from Arista, her co-star Kevin Costner; her music director Ricky Minor, her cousin Dionne Warwick and her bodyguard and brother-in-law Ray Watson, all spoke during the service. Aretha Franklin was listed on the programme as a singer, but on the day wasn't able to attend.

Bobby Brown was invited to the funeral and attended, but he left before the service began following a disagreement with security guards about seating.

Whitney was buried the following day on 19 February in Fairview Cemetery, in Westfield, New Jersey next to her father, John.

You Were Loved - Epilogue

Whitney lives on through her music and incredible legacy. Modern stars including Beyonce, Alicia Keys, Mary J Blige, Faith Evans, Mariah Carey, Lady Gaga, Celine Dion, Pink, Jennifer Hudson, Rihanna, Britney Spears and Adele have all acknowledged the influence Whitney had on their music and careers and credited her as an inspiration.

Since her death she has been inducted into the Rock and Roll Hall of Fame (2020), the National Recording Industry (2010 for *I Will Always Love You*), the Grammy Hall of Fame (2018), the R&B Music Hall of Fame, the Georgia Music Hall of Fame and the New Jersey Hall of Fame (2013).

The captivating performance style, powerhouse vocals and astonishing range that helped her smash into the annuls of pop history mean that she will never be forgotten.

Bobbi Kristina

Bobbi Kristina had been fighting her own battle with drugs and addiction since she was a teenager. Then in circumstances strangely similar to those in which Whitney died, she was found unconscious in a bath at her home in 2015. She was in a medically induced coma for six months and eventually died on 25 July 2015, aged just 22.

According to the medical examiner, cannabis and alcohol were found in her system, along with prescription medication for anxiety/and or depression, and the underlying cause of death was given as 'immersion associated with drug intoxication'.

Robyn Crawford

Robyn Crawford built a career outside the music business after leaving Whitney's crew. She worked for a time as a journalist and is now a fitness trainer. She is married and has adopted twins with her partner Lisa.

In 2019 she wrote a memoir entitled, *A Song For You* and in an interview with the BBC to promote the book said that she wanted to remind the world that Whitney was 'bighearted, unselfish, hilarious' and phenomenally talented.

'I want to elevate her. I want to lift her so she can hold her legacy up way high,' she said.

Sparkle

The official trailer for *Sparkle* was released on 2 April 2012 which brought mixed emotions for the film's producer Debra Martin Chase who said; 'On the one hand, I'm so excited about the movie and we're really happy with how it turned out. (But) just to have it said yet again that this is Whitney's last performance, it's hard. It's hard.' The film was eventually released in August 2012.

Bobby Brown

Bobby Brown married Alicia Etheredge in June 2012, after a two-year engagement. The couple have three children. In 2020, his eldest son, Bobby Brown Jnr, from his 11-year relationship with Kim Ward in the 80s and 90s, died aged 28. The autopsy report recorded that he had died from the effects of alcohol, cocaine and fentanyl.

Discography

Studio albums

Whitney Houston (1985)

Whitney (1987)

I'm Your Baby Tonight (1990)

My Love is Your Love (1998)

Just Whitney (2002)

One Wish (The Holiday Album) (2003)

I Look To You (2009)

Compilation albums

Whitney: The Greatest Hits (2000)

Love, Whitney (2001)

Artist Collection: Whitney Houston (2004)

The Ultimate Collection (2007)

The Essential Whitney Houston (2011)

I Will Always Love You: The Best of Whitney Houston (2012)

Soundtrack albums

The Bodyguard (1992)

The Preacher's Wife (1996)

Live albums

Whitney Houston Live: Her Greatest Performances (2014)

Singles

1980s

Hold Me (with Teddy Prendergrass)

Thinking About You

You Give Good Love

All At Once

Saving All My Love For You

How Will I Know

Didn't We Almost Have It All

So Emotional

Where Do Broken Hearts Go

Love Will Save the Day

One Moment In Time

I Know Him So Well

1990s

I'm Your Baby Tonight

All The Man That I Need

The Star Spangled Banner

Miracle

My Name Is Not Susan

I Belong To You

We Didn't Know

I Will Always Love You

I'm Every Woman

I Have Nothing

Run To You

Queen of the Night

Exhale (Shoop Shoop)

Count On Me

Why Does It Hurt So Bad

I Believe in You and Me

Step by Step
My Heart is Calling
When You Believe
Heartbreak Hotel
It's Not Right but It's Okay
My Love is Your Love
I Learned From The Best

2000s

Could I Have This Kiss Forever

If I Told You That
Same Script, Different Cast
Fine
The Star Spangled Banner (Re-release)
Whatchulookinat
One of Those Days
Try It On My Own
Love That Man
One Wish for Christmas
I Look To You
Million Dollar Bill

Posthumous releases

Celebrate

His Eye Is On The Sparrow

I Look To You

Memories

Higher Love

Do You Hear What I Hear?

Filmography

The Bodyguard (1992)

Waiting to Exhale (1995)

The Preacher's Wife (1996)

Cinderella (1997)

Sparkle (2012)

World tours

The Greatest Love World Tour (1986)

Moment of Truth World Tour (1987-88)

I'm Your Baby Tonight World Tour (1991)

The Bodyguard World Tour (1993-94)

My Love Is Your Love World Tour (1999)

Nothing But Love World Tour (2009-10)

Whitney's Awards

Whitney Houston holds the Guinness World Record for being the most awarded female artist of all time. Her 400-plus career prizes include six Grammy awards and 22 American Music Awards. She was nominated for many more - often in several categories each year, such was her versatility - and won the following:

1985

Billboard Number One Awards	New Black Artist
Billboard Number One Awards	New Pop Artist
The 18th NAACP Image Awards	Outstanding New Artist

1986

The 13th American Music Awards (Favourite Soul/R&B single)	*You Give Good Love*
The 13th American Music Awards (Favourite Soul/R&B video)	*Saving All My Love For You*
The 28th GRAMMY Awards (Best Pop Vocal Performance, Female)	*Saving All My Love For You*
Black Gold Awards	Outstanding New Female Vocalist
The NARM 1985-1986 Best Seller Awards (Best-selling Album by a New Artist)	*Whitney Houston*
The NARM 1985-1986 Best Seller Awards (Best-selling Black Music Album by a Female Artist)	*Whitney Houston*
The 3rd MTV Video Music Awards	*How Will I Know* (Best Female Video)
The 38th Emmy Awards (Outstanding Individual Performance in a Variety or Music Program)	for The 28th Annual Grammy Awards
Billboard – The Year In Music and Video	Top Pop Artist of the Year
Billboard - The Year in Music & Video	Top Pop Album (*Whitney Houston*)
Billboard - The Year in Music & Video	Top Pop Album Artist
Billboard - The Year in Music & Video	Top Pop Album Artist – Female
Billboard - The Year in Music & Video	Top Black Album (*Whitney Houston*)
Billboard - The Year in Music & Video	Top Black Album Artist
The 18th NAACP Image Awards	Outstanding Female Recording Artist

1987

The 14th American Music Awards	Favourite Pop/Rock Female Artist
The 14th American Music Awards	Favourite Pop/Rock Album (*Whitney Houston*)

The 14th American Music Awards	Favourite Soul/R&B Female Artist
The 14th American Music Awards	Favourite Soul/R&B Album (*Whitney Houston*)
The 14th American Music Awards	Favourite Soul/R&B Video Single (*Greatest Love of All*)
1987 BRIT Awards	Best International Solo Artist
The 13th People's Choice Awards	Favourite Female Musical Performer
1987 Billboard The Year in Music & Video	Top Pop Album Artist - Female
The 9th American Black Achievement Awards	The Music Award

1988

Rennbahn-Express Magazine's Starwhal	Golden Penguin Award - Best Female Singer
National Urban Coalition 1988	Distinguished Artist/Humanitarian
The 15th American Music Awards	Favourite Pop/Rock Female Artist
The 15th American Music Awards	Favourite Pop/Rock Single (*I Wanna Dance With Somebody (Who Loves Me)*)
The 30th GRAMMY Awards	Best Pop Vocal Performance, Female (*I Wanna Dance With Somebody (Who Loves Me)*)
The 14th People's Choice Awards	Favourite Female Musical Performer
The 2nd Soul Train Music Awards	Best R&B Album of the Year, Female (*Whitney*)
Grambling State University	Honorary
Doctorate of Humane Letters	
American Dental Hygienists' Association	America's Greatest Smiles
The 1st Garden State Music Awards	Best Female Vocalist, Rock/Pop
The 1st Garden State Music Awards	Best Album, Rock/Pop (*Whitney*)
The 1st Garden State Music Awards	Best Single, Rock/Pop (*So Emotional*)
The 1st Garden State Music Awards	Best Female Vocalist, R&B/Dance
The 1st Garden State Music Awards	Best Album, R&B/Dance (*Whitney*)
The 1st Garden State Music Awards	Best Single, R&B/Dance (So Emotional)
The 1st Garden State Music Awards	Best Music Video (*I Wanna Dance With Somebody (Who Loves Me)*)
Billboard The Year in Music & Video	Top Pop Singles Artist - Female
BRAVO Magazine's Bravo Otto	Best Female Singer - Silver Otto Award
The 10th American Black Achievement Awards	The Music Award

1989

The 16th American Music Awards	Favourite Pop/Rock Female Artist
The 16th American Music Awards	Favourite Soul/R&B Female Artist
The 15th People's Choice Awards	Favourite Female Musical Performer

1990

The 46th United Negro College Fund Awards	The Frederick D. Patterson Award

Points of Light	Points of Light Contributing Leader
The 21st Songwriters Hall of Fame Induction & Awards	Howie Richmond Hitmaker Award
The 4th Essence Awards	The Essence Award for the Performing Arts

1991

The 8th American Cinema Awards	The Musical Performer of the Year
The 13th American Black Achievement Awards	The Music Award
The 2nd Billboard Music Awards	Top R&B Artist
The 2nd Billboard Music Awards	Top R&B Album (*I'm Your Baby Tonight*)
The 2nd Billboard Music Awards	Top R&B Album Artist
The 2nd Billboard Music Awards	Top R&B Singles Artist

1992

The 13th CableACE Awards	**Performance in a Music Special or Series**
	(HBO Presents Welcome Home Heroes with Whitney Houston)
The 8th Carousel of Hope Ball	Brass Ring Award

1993

The 7th Japan Gold Disc Awards	Grand Prix Album Award, International
	(*The Bodyguard Soundtrack*)
The 7th Japan Gold Disc Awards	Compilation Album Prize, International
	(*The Bodyguard Soundtrack*)
The 7th Japan Gold Disc Awards	Grand Prix Single Award, International
	(*I Will Always Love You*)
Smash Hits Poll Winners Party	Best Female Artist
The 7th Soul Train Music Awards	Best R&B/Soul Single, Female (*I Will Always Love You*)
The 19th People's Choice Awards	Favourite Female Musical Performer
The 19th People's Choice Awards	Favourite New Music Video (*I Will Always Love You*)
The 2nd MTV Movie Awards	Best Song From A Movie (*I Will Always Love You*)
BRAVO Magazine's Bravo Otto	Best Actress - Silver Otto Award
BRAVO Magazine's Bravo Otto	Best Female Singer - Silver Otto Award
The 5th Billboard Music Awards	Hot 100 Singles Artist
The 5th Billboard Music Awards	Hot 100 Single (*I Will Always Love You*)
The 5th Billboard Music Awards	Hot R&B Singles Artist
The 5th Billboard Music Awards	Hot R&B Single (*I Will Always Love You*)
The 5th Billboard Music Awards	Top Billboard 200 Album (Top Album of the Year)
	(*The Bodyguard Soundtrack*)
The 5th Billboard Music Awards	Top R&B Album (*The Bodyguard Soundtrack*)
The 5th Billboard Music Awards	Top Soundtrack Album (*The Bodyguard Soundtrack*)
The 5th Billboard Music Awards	Album Most Weeks at #1 for 20 weeks
	(Special Award) (*The Bodyguard Soundtrack*)

The 5th Billboard Music Awards	Single Most Weeks at #1 for 14 weeks
	(Special Award) (*I Will Always Love You*)
The 5th Billboard Music Awards	#1 World Artist
The 5th Billboard Music Awards	#1 World Single *I Will Always Love You*

1994

The 8th Japan Gold Disc Awards	Special Award, International (*I Will Always Love You*)
The 8th Japan Gold Disc Awards	Special Award, International (*The Bodyguard Soundtrack*)
The 26th NAACP Image Awards	Entertainer of the Year
The 26th NAACP Image Awards	Outstanding Female Artist
The 26th NAACP Image Awards	Outstanding Album (*The Bodyguard Soundtrack*)
The 26th NAACP Image Awards	Outstanding Soundtrack Album, Film or TV
	(*The Bodyguard Soundtrack*)
The 26th NAACP Image Awards	Outstanding Music Video (*I'm Every Woman*)
The 21st American Music Awards	Favourite Soul/R&B Female Artist
The 21st American Music Awards	Favourite Adult Contemporary Album
	(*The Bodyguard Soundtrack*)
The 21st American Music Awards	Favourite Pop/Rock Album (*The Bodyguard Soundtrack*)
The 21st American Music Awards	Favourite Soul/R&B Single (*I Will Always Love You*)
The 21st American Music Awards	Favourite Soul/R&B Album (*The Bodyguard Soundtrack*)
The 21st American Music Awards	Favourite Pop/Rock Female Artist
The 21st American Music Awards	Favourite Pop/Rock Single (*I Will Always Love You*)
The 21st American Music Awards	Award of Merit (Special Award)
1994 BRIT Awards	Best Soundtrack/Cast Recording
	(*The Bodyguard Soundtrack*)
The 36th GRAMMY Awards	Album of the Year (*The Bodyguard Soundtrack*)
The 36th GRAMMY Awards	Record of the Year (*I Will Always Love You*)
The 36th GRAMMY Awards	Best Pop Vocal Performance, Female (*I Will Always Love You*)
The 8th Soul Train Music Awards	Sammy Davis, Jr. Award as Entertainer of the Year
The 8th Soul Train Music Awards	Best R&B Song of the Year (*I Will Always Love You*)
The 24th Juno Awards	Best Selling Album - Foreign or Domestic
	(*The Bodyguard Soundtrack*)
The NARM 1993-1994 Best Seller Awards	Best-selling Soundtrack (*The Bodyguard Soundtrack*)
The NABOB 10th Communications Awards	Entertainer of the Year
The 15th American Black Achievement Awards	The Music Award
The 6th World Music Awards	World's Best-Selling Overall Recording Artist
The 6th World Music Awards	World's Best Selling Pop Artist of the Year
The 6th World Music Awards	World's Best Selling R&B Artist of the Year
The 6th World Music Awards	World's Best-Selling American Recording Artist of the Year
The 6th World Music Awards	World's Best Selling Female Recording Artist of the Era
Harris Poll (Harris Interactive)	#1 Favourite Singer/Musician or Musical Group

1995

The 2nd VH1 Honors	VH1 Honors Award
Soul Train 25th Anniversary Hall Of Fame	Inductee
The 2nd International Achievement in Arts Awards	Distinguished Achievement in Music and Film/Video

1996

The 10th Soul Train Music Awards	Best R&B/Soul Single, Female (*Exhale (Shoop Shoop)*)
The NARM 1995-1996 Best Seller Awards	Best-selling Soundtrack Recording (*Waiting To Exhale Soundtrack*)
The 27th NAACP Image Awards	Outstanding Motion Picture (*Waiting To Exhale*)
The 27th NAACP Image Awards	Outstanding Female Artist (*Exhale (Shoop Shoop)*)
The 27th NAACP Image Awards	Outstanding Song (*Exhale (Shoop Shoop)*)
The 27th NAACP Image Awards	Outstanding Soundtrack Album (*Waiting To Exhale Soundtrack*)
The 27th NAACP Image Awards	Outstanding Album (*Waiting To Exhale Soundtrack*)
The 2nd BET Walk of Fame	Inductee
The 12th Carousel of Hope Ball	High Hopes Award
The 7th Billboard Music Awards	Soundtrack Album of the Year (*Waiting to Exhale Soundtrack*)

1997

The 24th American Music Awards	Favourite Adult Contemporary Artist
The 28th NAACP Image Awards	Outstanding Lead Actress in a Motion Picture (*The Preacher's Wife*)
The 28th NAACP Image Awards	Outstanding Gospel Artist (for *The Preacher's Wife*)
The 28th NAACP Image Awards	Outstanding Album (*The Preacher's Wife Soundtrack*)
The NARM 1996-1997 Best Seller Awards	Best-selling Gospel Recording (*The Preacher's Wife Soundtrack*)
The 3rd Blockbuster Entertainment Awards	Favourite Female, R&B (*The Preacher's Wife Soundtrack*)
The 28th Dove Awards	Outstanding Mainstream Contribution to Gospel Music
The 10th Essence Awards	The Triumphant Spirit Award
The 12th ASCAP Film & Television Music Awards	Most Performed Songs, Motion Pictures (Count On Me)
The 14th ASCAP Pop Awards	ASCAP Pop Award (Count On Me)

1998

The 24th People's Choice Awards	Favourite Female Musical Performer (tied with Reba McEntire)
The 6th Trumpet Awards	The Pinnacle Award
The 12th Soul Train Music Awards	The Quincy Jones Award for Outstanding Career Achievements in the field of entertainment
The 29th Dove Awards	Best Traditional Gospel Recorded Song (*I Go to The Rock*)

1999

The 30th NAACP Image Awards	Outstanding Duo or Group (*When You Believe* - Duet with Mariah Carey
Brazil Dance Music Award	Best International Female
Deirdre O'Brien Child Advocacy Centre	Child Advocate of the Year
Recording Industry Association of America	Top-selling R&B Female Artist of the Century
Recording Industry Association of America	Top-selling Soundtrack Album of the Century (*The Bodyguard Soundtrack*)
1999 MTV Europe Music Awards	Best R&B
1999 Bambi Verleihung	Pop International

2000

The 1st HMV Harlem Walk of Fame	Inductee
2000 Edison Music Awards	Best Singer, International (*My Love Is Your Love*)
The 15th International Dance Music Awards	Best Pop 12 in Dance Record (*It's Not Right But It's Okay*)
The 1st NRJ Music Awards	International Album of the Year (*My Love Is Your Love*)
The 31st NAACP Image Awards	Outstanding Female Artist (*Heartbreak Hotel* featuring Faith Evans and Kelly Price)
The 42nd GRAMMY Awards	Best Female R&B Vocal Performance (*It's Not Right But It's Okay*)
The 14th Soul Train Music Awards	The Artist of the Decade - Female, for extraordinary artistic contributions during the 1990s

2001

The 16th Japan Gold Disc Awards	Pop Album of the Year – International (*Whitney: The Greatest Hits*)
2001 Meteor Ireland Music Awards	Best International Female (*Whitney: The Greatest Hits*)
The 1st BET Awards	BET Lifetime Achievement Award

2004

The 1st Women's World Awards	World Arts Award for Lifetime Achievement
The 6th CCTV-MTV Music Honors	International Outstanding Achievement

2005

MTV's Greatest Voices in Music	Ranked No 3

2006

Guinness World Records	Most consecutive US # 1 Singles
Guinness World Records	Most consecutive weeks at #1 on UK singles chart (solo female)
Guinness World Records	Most consecutive weeks at #1 on US singles chart (solo female)
Guinness World Records	Most cumulative weeks at #1 on US singles chart (solo female individual single)
The New Jersey Walk of Fame	Inductee

2009

The 37th American Music Awards	International Artist Award

2010

The 3rd BET Honors	The BET Honor for Entertainment
The 41st NAACP Image Awards	Outstanding Music Video (*I Look To You*)

2012

Billboard Music Awards	Billboard Millennium Award
Guinness World Records	Most Simultaneous Hits in UK
Guinness World Records	Highest Trending Google Search
Guinness World Records	Best-selling single by a female artist (US)
Guinness World Records	Biggest-selling soundtrack album
Guinness World Records	First recipient of the BET Lifetime Achievement Award
2012 MTV Europe Music Awards	Global Icon Award
2012 Soul Train Music Awards	Best Gospel/Inspirational Performance (*Celebrate* - Duet with Jordin Sparks)

2013

Grammy Awards	Grammy Hall of Fame
Barbados Music Awards	International Icon Award
The 44th NAACP Image Awards	Best Song (*I Look To You* - Duet with R. Kelly)
The 44th NAACP Image Awards	Outstanding Album
	(*I Will Always Love You: The Best Of Whitney Houston*)
Georgia Music Hall of Fame	Inductee
ABC Greatest Women in Music	Rank # 1
The Singers Hall of Fame	Inductee

2014-18

New Jersey Hall of Fame	Inductee
Vevo Certified Awards	+100,000,000 views on Vevo (*I Will Always Love You*)
R&B Music Hall of Fame	Inductee
The Official Charts Pop Gem Hall of Fame	Inductee
Vevo Certified Awards	+ 100 million views (*I Have Nothing*)
Vevo Certified Awards	+ 100 million views (*When You Believe* ft Mariah Carey)
Vevo Certified Awards	+ 100 million views (*I Look To You*)
Vevo Certified Awards	+ 100 million views (*I Wanna Dance With Somebody*)
Vevo Certified Awards	+ 100 million views (*Run To You*)
Vevo Certified Awards	+ 100 million views (*Greatest Love Of All*)
Vevo 10x Certified Awards	+ I billion views (*I Will Always Love You*)

2018-

Grammy Hall of Fame	Inductee (I Will Always Love You)
National Recording Registry	Inductee (I Will Always Love You)
Rock & Roll Hall of Fame (2020)	Inductee